exploring

HEAVENLY PLACES

STRATEGIES FOR THIS PRESENT BATTLE

VOLUME 11

For we do not wrestle against flesh and blood, but against the rulers, against the authorities, against the cosmic powers over this present darkness, against the spiritual forces of evil in the heavenly places.
Ephesians 6:12

exploring

HEAVENLY PLACES

STRATEGIES FOR THIS PRESENT BATTLE

VOLUME 11

BY

Paul L Cox

Barbara Kain Parker

EXPLORING HEAVENLY PLACES, VOLUME 11
STRATEGIES FOR THIS PRESENT BATTLE

By Paul L Cox and Barbara Kain Parker

Aslan's Place Publications
9315 Sagebrush Street
Apple Valley, CA 92308
760-810-0990
www.aslansplace.com

Unless otherwise indicated, scriptures are taken from: The ESV® Bible (The Holy Bible, English Standard Version®) copyright © 2001 by Crossway Bible, a publishing ministry of Good News Publishers. Used by permission. All rights reserved.

Some scripture quotations are from the: New King James Version (NKJV): New King James Version®. Copyright © 1982 by Thomas Nelson. Used by permission. All rights reserved.

ISBN 978-1-0861-8512-6

Printed in the United States of America

TABLE OF CONTENTS

INTRODUCTION

Driving home to California from Colorado in late August, my husband and I decided to take a route that wound through Rocky Mountain National Park where the scenery is spectacular. The higher we climbed into the mountains, the colder it got; the farther we progressed, the slower the traffic crawled as we crossed the Continental Divide. It was only a two-lane road at the time, and the drop-off on either side seemed incredibly steep and a bit scary; a smattering of snow already covered the barren, above-the-tree-line ground on either side, and the road was very icy. As that snow first increased and then eventually melted, each flake would join the watershed; on one side it would flow to the right and the other to the left. Snowflakes that once fell only inches apart would move in opposite directions, soon to become separated by miles and miles and miles on their journey to the sea.

The Continental Divide seems as good an illustration as any to portray the stark division we see all around us. We tend to label our political differences as right versus left, or conservative versus liberal; issues of faith become Christianity versus Islam, New Age and all manner of idolatry; populations become citizens versus immigrants, or one culture pitted against another; and the list goes on. Seemingly, it gets very complicated; which side of what should we be on? Who is right and who is wrong? But reality is really very simple to define: our division, our battle, is the age-old struggle of rebellion and lawlessness versus God's standards of righteousness and justice:

> *Righteousness and justice are the foundation of Your throne; Lovingkindness and truth go before You.*[1]

The truth is that each person has a choice:

> *And if it is evil in your eyes to serve the Lord, choose this day whom you will serve, whether the gods your fathers served in the region*

beyond the River, or the gods of the Amorites in whose land you dwell. But as for me and my house, we will serve the Lord.[2]

In the United States, recent events (at the time of this writing) have provided one example after another of the divisiveness that is evident:

- Our midterm elections starkly highlighted the national split as an array of candidates ranging from ultra-left socialists to ultra-right constitutionalists campaigned and won or lost their respective offices. Sadly, the competition was not conducted with any level of respect between rivals.

- The tragic shootings at a Jewish synagogue in Pittsburg, PA, followed months later by another one in Poway, CA, took the lives of twelve people; and public reaction ranged from grief and prayers of support, to anti-Semitism, to a war of words regarding who was at fault in each case.

- Only days after the Pittsburg shooting, we awoke to the terrible news of another shooting incident, this time at the Borderline Bar and Grill in Thousand Oaks, CA; twelve people were killed by a shooter who was a highly decorated Marine Corp veteran, and blame game began immediately.

Those three examples represent only the smallest fraction of the divisiveness within our nation, and it's clear that the international conflicts among humanity are off the charts. Unfortunately, there are few who recognize either the true battle that rages on or its scope. The victory of righteousness over evil did occur about two thousand years ago at Jesus' crucifixion in Jerusalem, but even among Christians the mystery of what that entails still evades anything beyond the most basic understanding of redemption and salvation. Why? Because even many believers have been as blinded by sin as those who do not believe; even those who see themselves as dedicated Christians often remain bound up in traditions and doctrinal squabbles that have nothing at all to do with God's truth. The enemy has so effectively dealt out his cards of deception that there is a terrible lack of awareness in the Church regarding the access we have in the here-and-now (as opposed to the sweet by-and-by) to the heavenly realms, which is actually where the frontlines of this battle exist.

Going back to the Thousand Oaks tragedy, Lt. Col Damon Friedman, founder of SOF Missions, has been quoted as saying:

> Overall fitness, which is comprised of physical, psychological and spiritual components, is key to healing. We have made significant advancements in caring for our warriors with visible wounds, but we continue to lack in addressing the invisible wounds. In order to make advancements in overall fitness we must take a systematic and holistic approach. Spiritual fitness is key to addressing moral injury, reestablishing identity and helping the warrior along their path to wellness. The fact is, when it comes to spiritual fitness only God can heal certain wounds.[3]

So true, and it applies not only to wounded warriors from the military, but also to wounded people from every walk of life. Only God is able to sort out this whole divisive mess, but as His representatives on earth we can enter into the battle armed with His authority and His strength. This is the reason for this volume of our *Exploring Heavenly Places* series:

> *For we do not wrestle against flesh and blood, but against the rulers, against the authorities, against the cosmic powers over this present darkness, against the spiritual forces of evil in the heavenly places.*[4]

We have chosen our side in the oh-so-real conflict between God and His righteousness and justice versus all that is evil; we oppose all that is evil and rebellious in the world. Our prayer is that this book will help equip you for the battle, and that you will join us in the fight.

Paul L. Cox
Barbara Kain Parker

[1] Psalm 89:14

[2] Joshua 24:15

[3] https://www.charismanews.com/us/73960-greg-laurie-reveals-the-most-significant-factor-in-these-shootings

[4] Ephesians 6:12

CHAPTER ONE

WE ARE AT WAR

I (Paul) have stories: oh my, do I have stories!

Standing at the pharmacy counter waiting for my prescription to be filled, I felt a sharp pain in my back. Turning around, I realized a man was holding a gun against my back and threatening, "This is a holdup; go behind the counter and get on your knees." Clearly, this was not a time for a discussion so I obediently followed his instructions and knelt down. He bound my wrists together behind my back and must have been kidding as he remarked, "This must be your first time being tied up and held at gunpoint." I was not amused! My only thought was, "I am going to heaven now, but this will ruin Donna's Christmas." After what seemed like hours, the thieves finally left and I was untied; police reports were filed; and I returned home, realizing it was too late to go out with missionary friends who were visiting. As I opened our door, Donna asked, "Why are you so late?" "My reply, "I guess you can say I was held up."

A candidate vetting process preceded our ministry at Bethany Baptist Church in Montclair, CA. Meanwhile, our daughter, Corrie, was staying with Donna's parents. As this was such a very important event in our lives, the added stress over our daughter's trials during our absence was most unwelcome! First, she fell off a wagon and experienced a concussion. Then, the afternoon following my first sermon, I was notified during a church meeting that Corrie had been riding her tricycle and caught her hand between the handlebar and the bottom of the hot BBQ, which resulted in severe burns.

I was conducting a funeral for a man who had been divorced; but his ex-wife was there and I could tell that she was really agitated. To put this in context I should explain that before a pastor ministers at a funeral you get a little card that lists the people who are survivors of the deceased; ex-wives are not included on that list. The following Saturday night, I got a call asking the time of the Sunday service. I wondered, "Is this the lady from that funeral service?" because somehow, I had a check in my spirit that there was going to be a problem the next day. At the end of the Sunday morning service, I saw a woman step into the sanctuary and sit down on the back pew; and yes, it was the ex-wife who was unhappy with me for not mentioning her name. I received word from an usher that she wanted to talk to me, so I called out to the congregation asking for several "strong and tall men" to come to the front. I instructed them to surround me as I walked to the back of the sanctuary and stood before her saying, "Ok, I'll talk to you." She became violently angry and started throwing things all over the place. The men grabbed me and whisked me back down the aisle and into to my office; Donna and the kids were bought there too. We were told to not go home, but to go instead to a friend's house while the police were summoned. I found out later that after I left, she hit a young girl and the father confronted the lady, which resulted in heightened drama. Then, the ex-wife had driven up and down the aisles of the parking lot, shouting curses and contemptuous words against me out of her window, letting the world know what a terrible person I was.

A few months later, I received a call during a deacon's meeting that all of the police in Montclair were at our house. A person who had murdered someone in a neighboring town had gained access into the new addition we were adding. I was told to remain calm because a police officer was guarding my family in our hallway while the rest of the police were trying to get this man out of our addition. I left the deacon's meeting and arrived home, only to find a police blockade that I was not allowed to cross because it was considered an active crime scene. I watched as the police pursued a man out of our side yard and down the street; police dogs chased him until he was driven up a tree.

A few more months passed before I received a call from someone who said, "Do you know that the police have received a message saying that a man is coming after you with a gun?" My response was, "Well that's nice," and I went to bed; but Donna remained up on the counter in the bathroom, watching out the window while I am slept.

Another time, a lady, a member who lived across the street from our church, had been very kind to us. We had enjoyed a meal at her house, but somehow found her very strange. One day when the Santa Ana winds were blowing, she came pounding on the church's office doors demanding, "Where is Paul Cox? When I went to sleep it wasn't windy, but now it's windy! Where is this supposed man of God?" She continued pounding and shouting, "Where is this man of God?" But because there was a preschool and elementary school at the church, lockdown procedures were followed and she was unable to find me at the church. Then she decided to walk to my home but was not sure where I lived, so she knocked on several doors along our street while shouting, "Where is this man of God?" Finally, she arrived at our door. We locked it, got everyone into the hallway again, and called the police. They captured her, and she was handcuffed and taken away under Code 5150.[1] After her release, she continued to call our house dozens of times an hour, day after day after day.

There was another trial with our daughter, Corrie. She became sick with mononucleosis in the sixth grade and suffered for almost two years. During that time, our phone apparently started dialing 911 all on its own; the police would respond, and we would assure them that no one had called. After many such episodes, the police began warning us that we would be in serious trouble if these false calls did not stop. It was only after several weeks that a problem was discovered with the 911 system and it was revealed that we were not responsible for all of those false alarms.

After I had resigned from the church, we were watching TV in our home and heard a very loud explosion that was definitely not a part of the program. We headed outside and were startled to find that a bomb had gone off and damaged one of our cars. Again, the police were called and the bomb squad soon arrived. An investigation determined that a small group of teenagers that had been a part of the church had constructed a homemade bomb out of a liter bottle and explosive ingredients.

14

How was it possible for so many bizarre things to happen to us? I was very close to other pastors, and none of their lives were filled with so much drama; I was not prepared for this! Why was this happening? Then I had a thought, "Perhaps the enemy has anticipated what we are going to do, and all these things that are happening to us are attempts to block us from pursuing God's call on our life." Then the realization came: We are at war!

This really was a new concept for me. In the realm of the pastors and churches that I knew, I did not hear much about any spiritual battle because many Christians hold to the view that since the cross the battle is over. Jesus has won; therefore, we have won; end of story. Unfortunately, this is not a biblical view. Yes, Jesus definitely has secured the final victory at the cross, but we are to engage in confronting the enemy and are instructed to take back regions that were given away at the fall.

This is the nature of our life! It is a war, and we are to engage with our Commander in Chief, the Lord Jesus Christ, to confront evil in our lives, our family's lives and in co-operation with others in ministry to the world around us. Regrettably, non-Christians, and many Christians alike, do not comprehend the reality of the Christian walk. How many actually view life like Dustin Hoffman's father did?

> Hoffman shares a birthday with his father, and recently spoke about a conversation they had when he was 50 and his father 80. "We were walking on the beach," said Hoffman." "And I said, 'Dad, you're 80 today. And I'm 50. Do you have any words you can give me?' And he said, 'Yeah, it's all bull****.' And he turned around and walked away." [2]

Tragic! Life is to be lived for Jesus Christ in order to see His Kingdom established on the earth; we are to struggle to see our lives become conformed to the image of Christ. The process is a battle that must be fought from His place of rest, in a life that is filled with His joy and peace. We live for Him, and we battle for and with Him.

Many years ago, I came across a book called *God at War* by Gregory Boyd, who is a Princeton graduate and the pastor of Woodland Hills Church in Minnesota. When he examined the Bible, he came to the same conclusion that we are at war:

> The Bible as well as the early post apostolic Church assumes that the creation is caught up in the crossfire of an age-old cosmic battle between good and evil. As in other warfare worldviews, the Bible assumes that the course of this warfare greatly affects life on earth.[3]

> Hostile, evil, cosmic forces that are seeking to destroy God's beneficent plan for the cosmos have, in fact, seized God's good creation. God wages war against these forces, however, and through the person of Jesus Christ has now secured the overthrow of this evil cosmic army. The Church as the Body of Christ has been called to be a decisive means by which this final overthrow is to be carried out.[4]

> Thus, the Christian life is for Paul a life of spiritual military service. It is about being a good soldier (2 Tim 2:4), about "fighting the good fight" (1 Tim 1:18; 6:12), about "waging war" (2 Cor 10:3), and about "struggling" with a cosmic enemy (Eph. 6:12). Given his view of the ever-present reality of Satan and his kingdom, and given his understanding of what Christ was about and what the church is supposed to be about, it is hard to see how [Paul] could have viewed the Christian life differently.[5]

> Despite Christ's victory, the New Testament continues to define the Christian life in warfare terms. The outcome of the war is settled, but there are still important battles to be fought. Fighting them is what the Christian life is all about... The confidence and hope of the believer in all of this is that Christ has once and for all time vanquished the enemy, and that someday this victory over Satan and the cessation of all the evil that flows from him shall be perfectly manifested.[6]

The Bible says we are at war; life confirms that we are at war. So, what is our response? We follow our Commander in Chief into the battle, putting on the full armor of God,[7] waging war against the generational issues that have pushed against us, and walking in the blessings and freedom that we need to rule and reign with our Lord Jesus Christ.

---

[1] California law code for the temporary, involuntary psychiatric commitment of individuals who present a danger to themselves or others due to signs of mental illness.

[2] https://www.gq-magazine.co.uk/article/dustin-hoffman-interview

[3] Boyd, Gregory. God at War. p. 18

[4] Ibid. p. 19.

[5] Ibid. p. 282

[6] Ibid. p. 290-291

[7] Ephesians 6:10-20

CHAPTER TWO

A CALL TO ENLIST AND ENDURE

Have you ever looked at any military recruiting ads? Most that I've (Barbara) seen have been designed to lure a prospective soldier with promises of career advancement, international travel, action and adventure. In a way, we could say that Jesus was recruiting for His own army, so what enticements did He use? Not exactly those one would expect:

> *These twelve Jesus sent out, instructing them, "Go nowhere among the Gentiles and enter no town of the Samaritans, but go rather to the lost sheep of the house of Israel. And proclaim as you go, saying, 'The kingdom of heaven is at hand.' Heal the sick, raise the dead, cleanse lepers, cast out demons. You received without paying; give without pay. Acquire no gold or silver or copper for your belts, no bag for your journey, or two tunic or sandals or a staff, for the laborer deserves his food…Behold, I am sending you out as sheep in the midst of wolves, so be wise as serpents and innocent as doves. Beware of men, for they will deliver you over to courts and flog you in their synagogues, and you will be dragged before governors and kings for my sake, to bear witness before them and the Gentiles. When they deliver you over, do not be anxious how you are to speak or what you are to say, for what you are to say will be given to you in that hour. For it is not you who speak, but the Spirit of your Father speaking through you. Brother will deliver brother over to death, and the father his child, and children will rise against parents and have them put to death, and you will be hated by all for my name's sake. But the one who endured to the end will be saved."* [1]

Hmmm, seems like it might be smart to think twice about making such a commitment; just look at the implied threats! Sheep in the midst of wolves is guaranteed to become a sure-fire skirmish in which the sheep lose big time; the mission is to engage in exploits that defy human understanding, but there's no guarantee of financial resources or personal comforts; much wisdom is required, but one must remain totally selfless and innocent-yet-vulnerable before people who will not only be as hateful as possible but will also ridicule, beat up, and haul you off to court; oh, and they might just kill you too.

But before walking away too quickly, just look at the perks. The Holy Spirit will be your personal speechwriter, and anyone who endures the battle will live eternally. Sounds like a pretty good deal to me because our Commander is the Lord, the One who suffered even more for us than He requires of us; the One, in fact, who gave His life so we may live. Our willingness to become embroiled in the war has everything to do with our devotion to God and our hatred of all evil that opposes Him; it's not about us, it's about Him because He deserves all the glory:

> *Worthy are you, our Lord and God, to receive glory and honor and power, for you created all things, and by your will they existed and were created.*[2]

We have been called to active duty in the Lord's army, and the battle is fierce:

> *But understand this, that in the last days there will come times of difficulty. For people will be lovers of self, lovers of money, proud, arrogant, abusive, disobedient to their parents, ungrateful, unholy, heartless, unappeasable, slanderous, without self-control, brutal, not loving good, treacherous, reckless, swollen with conceit, lovers of pleasure rather than lovers of God, having the appearance of godliness, but denying its power. Avoid such people. For among them are those who creep into households and capture weak women, burdened with sins and led astray by various passions, always learning and never able to arrive at a knowledge of the truth.*[3]

It's nothing new, for rebellion against God escalates on every hand, especially in these last days; but we are called to endure:

Share in suffering as a good soldier of Christ Jesus. No soldier gets entangled in civilian pursuits, since his aim is to please the one who enlisted him... The saying is trustworthy, for: If we have died with him, we will also live with him; if we endure, we will also reign with him; if we deny him, he also will deny us; if we are faithless, he remains faithful—for he cannot deny himself.[4]

If anyone is to be taken captive, to captivity he goes; if anyone is to be slain with the sword, with the sword must he be slain. Here is a call for the endurance of the saints, those who keep the commandments of God and their faith in Jesus.[5]

Satan and his cohorts have long been aware that to have any chance of holding onto their power requires extraordinary cunning and devious battle strategies because God is one tough opponent. The last thing they want are Christians who understand who they are; revealed sons of God who have finally realized the power and authority that is available through Jesus. In the Sermon on the Mount, He taught:

But seek first the kingdom of God and his righteousness, and all these things will be added to you. "Therefore do not be anxious about tomorrow, for tomorrow will be anxious for itself. Sufficient for the day is its own trouble.[6]

This truth remains as valid now as it was then, but is so simple that we often miss it. *Seek him first.* It means just what it says, so it shouldn't be a complicated or difficult-to-understand instruction. After all, the concept of diligently seeking after something is not foreign to us. If we desire the love and attention of another person we go after it with everything we've got—romantic dinners, gifts, doing all of the little things that would please the object of our affection. If it's a career, we perform and perform and perform to keep the boss happy—late hours, heavy workloads, compromised ethics—whatever it takes to get that bigger check or promotion; or sometimes to simply avoid being fired. We understand these pursuits, but when the Lord says, "Seek me first," we just don't get it; we don't seem to understand that the need to pursue Him is more important than any other endeavor.

And what of His admonition not to worry about tomorrow? After all, worry is such a normal part of life; it's so easy to do (no lessons required!), and who among us doesn't worry about something? Besides, aren't we supposed to worry about our kids, our health, or our finances? Aren't we supposed to worry about threatening global issues? No. Regardless of the worry, God is still our ultimate solution. Since His word remains true, and He promised that if we seek Him first all of our needs would be supplied, worry should have no place in our lives.

So why is such a simple truth so hard to implement? I believe it's largely because Satan knows how to manipulate us, and worry is just another face of fear. So, as I ponder the fact that God's perfect love casts out all fear,[7] I must conclude that fear is nothing more than Satan's weapon to immobilize us and prevent us from warring against him. In fact, fear just may be one of the biggest weapons in his arsenal.

The Lord gave me a picture of Satan sitting down with his generals for a planning session to figure out a battle strategy that would annihilate the people of God. Their voices reasoned:

> "What is a preventative measure we can take to keep people from experiencing God?"

> "Aha! Don't let them get saved in the first place."

> "How do we do that?"

> "Well, let's see, salvation happens only one way, by faith; so we have to destroy faith."

> "With doubt," cried one.

> "Yes, but what if their questions and objections can be answered?" replies another.

> "How about keeping them busy so they don't have time to think about God? Get them so involved in good causes that they forget to consult Him."

"That'd work on a lot of them, but in a moment of rest they might focus on Him just long enough to believe what He says."

On and on they go, carefully considering each of their weapons. Then a slimy little guy at the end speaks up, "How about using me? I'm insidious; I'm not even recognized for who I am, and I can get in and strike quietly. Before they know it, I've overtaken everything like an unseen cancer; I can disable them."

"Yes!" exclaims Satan himself. "Fear it is! Let's go for fear of how they'll have to change if they believe God; then add in fear of failure, fear of loss, fear of pain, fear of success, fear of responsibility; and oh, don't forget fear of death. Then, even if they do believe we can still control them. Through fear we can introduce frustration, pain, doubt, and a host of others. No one will even know the root is fear, so they won't be able to combat it. They'll be so busy trying to overcome such symptoms as anxiety, worry, phobias, jealousy and panic, that they'll be destroyed by the disease of fear."

There's no question that life is hard; we routinely face painful and difficult situations every day, so when fear wears the disguise of worry it often seems legitimate—sometimes even admirable. It dresses itself up to look like concern for things that are truly our responsibility or that directly affect us such as the financial stability of our family, the wellbeing of our children, health challenges, relationship issues, etc. And as if all of that isn't bad enough, Jesus warned us that before His return:

There will be signs in sun and moon and stars, and on the earth distress of nations in perplexity because of the roaring of the sea and the waves, people fainting with fear and with foreboding of what is coming on the world. For the powers of the heavens will be shaken.[8]

The picture often seems bleak, but when worry appears, fear has done its job; it has turned our attention away from the simplicity of God's command focused it onto the what-ifs of life. On top of that, each individual's fears seem to be personalized and custom fit to such a degree that living without them seems impossible. It's not though, because the scriptures repeatedly advise us to fear not, and God's definitely not going to advise us to do something that cannot be achieved.

> *I will not leave you as orphans; I will come to you... But the Helper, the Holy Spirit, whom the Father will send in my name, he will teach you all things and bring to your remembrance all that I have said to you. Peace I leave with you; my peace I give to you. Not as the world gives do I give to you. Let not your hearts be troubled, neither let them be afraid.*[9]

Our lack of immunity to the disease of fear may stem from many causes, one of which is that it's generational. An even more troubling scenarios is that we've simply taken the Lord's admonitions not to be afraid with a grain of salt because we simply cannot imagine a life without worry or fear. But regardless of the cause, Jesus is still the solution, regardless of the enemy's dirty tricks and powerful strategies. Having taken some big hits from him I do take heed of the warning:

> *Be sober-minded; be watchful. Your adversary the devil prowls around like a roaring lion, seeking someone to devour.*[10]

Just because we reject fear doesn't change the ferocity of the ongoing battle, but the truth is on our side. The strongest warrior was pre-determined in the Garden of Eden; we know Him Jesus:

> *I will put enmity between you and the woman, and between your offspring and her offspring; he shall bruise your head, and you shall bruise his heel.*[11]

Think about it for a second; a foot wound might disable you a bit, but a head wound will kill you, so Satan's fate has been sealed and he has a limited amount of time left to try to win a war that is already over except for the shouting:

Therefore God has highly exalted him and bestowed on him the name that is above every name, so that at the name of Jesus every knee should bow, in heaven and on earth and under the earth, and every tongue confess that Jesus Christ is Lord, to the glory of God the Father.[12]

Contrary to popular opinion, God remains in charge; He makes the rules. Satan's actions have limits set by God and he must stay within those guidelines:

Why do the nations rage and the peoples plot in vain? He who sits in the heavens laughs; the Lord holds them in derision. Then he will speak to them in his wrath, and terrify them in his fury, saying, "As for me, I have set my King on Zion, my holy hill."[13]

And the Lord said to Satan, "Behold, all that he has is in your hand. Only against him do not stretch out your hand." So Satan went out from the presence of the Lord… And the Lord said to Satan, "Behold, he is in your hand; only spare his life."[14]

Clearly, God is able to set us free, and fear needs to go if we are to be warriors in the Lord's army. The question though, is whether or not we are willing, because it is not an easy war; it is a spiritual conflict that takes place in unseen dimensions and we engage enemy combatants that are invisible to the human eye. That said, if we choose to fight, we can rest in His astounding promises:

What then shall we say to these things? If God is for us, who can be against us? He who did not spare his own Son but gave him up for us all, how will he not also with him graciously give us all things? Who shall bring any charge against God's elect? It is God who justifies. Who is to condemn? Christ Jesus is the one who died—more than that, who was raised—who is at the right hand of God, who indeed is interceding for us. Who shall separate us from the love of Christ? Shall tribulation, or distress, or persecution, or famine, or nakedness, or danger, or sword? As it is written, "For your sake we are being killed all the day long; we are regarded as sheep to be slaughtered." No, in all these things we are more than conquerors through him who loved us. For I am sure that neither death nor life, nor angels nor rulers, nor things present nor things to come, nor powers, nor height nor depth, nor anything else in all creation, will be able to separate us from the love of God in Christ Jesus our Lord.

Let's go back to that initial 'recruitment ad' from Jesus but take it just a step farther. Immediately after those stringent job requirements, He added:

So <u>have no fear of them</u>, for nothing is covered that will not be revealed, or hidden that will not be known. What I tell you in the dark, say in the light, and what you hear whispered, proclaim on the housetops. And <u>do not fear those who kill the body but cannot kill the soul</u>. Rather fear him who can destroy both soul and body in hell. Are not two sparrows sold for a penny? And not one of them will fall to the ground apart from your Father. But even the hairs of your head are all numbered. <u>Fear not</u>, therefore; you are of more value than many sparrows. So everyone who acknowledges me before men, I also will acknowledge before my Father who is in heaven, but whoever denies me before men, I also will deny before my Father who is in heaven.

Have no fear, do not fear, fear not, it is possible.[15] So yes, I'm in; sign me up Lord! How about you?

---

[1] Matthew 10:5-10, 16-22

[2] Revelation 4:11

[3] 2 Timothy 3:1-7

[4] 2 Timothy 2:3-4, 11-13

[5] Revelation 13:10a, 14:12

[6] Matthew 6:33-34

[7] 1 John 5:18

[8] Luke 21:25-26

[9] John 14:18, 26-27

[10] 1 Peter 5:8

[11] Genesis 3:15

[12] Philippians 2:9-11

[13] Psalm 2:1, 4-6

[14] Job 1:12, 2:6

[15] *Prayer to Abolish Fear* is available in Appendix 1

CHAPTER THREE

GO ON OFFENSE!

Watching our (Barbara) grandson's soccer game, we cheered as his team moved down the field on offense; they had the ball and were headed toward the goal. But whenever the other team gained possession, it was nail-biting-time and our cheers turned to groans. So it goes in any contest for every struggle involves both defensive and offensive positions and strategies; how much better to be on offense!

It seems that the Church has been playing defense throughout most of its history, so perhaps it's time to change our tactical engagement plan. Our minds understand that nothing can stand against the Lord, so why don't we use that knowledge to attack instead of continually striving either to deal with the fallout from the enemy's latest assault or to dig into a defensive position?

Often, our offensive weapons of war are not those that would ever be considered by the world, but then we are not of this world[1], are we? Hopefully, the remainder of this book will help equip our readers with 'otherworldly' scriptural tactics and strategies, beginning with a few well-known truths that may go unrecognized and under-utilized in this present battle.

'Hurry up and wait' is a common and not-always-humorous description of time being of the essence, but nothing can be accomplished because of an interminable wait. The term is thought to have originated in the military,[2] and illustrates the irony of rushing like mad to get somewhere or do something, only to be held hostage by unavoidable delays and unforeseen circumstances. Rarely do we enjoy waiting and it's natural to want to sped up the process, a dangerous tactic for well-meaning Christians who want to jump right into a situation and fix it for righteousness' sake. But being too hasty can complicate rather than help because we often end up acting out of our own strength instead of the Lord's. His ways are not our ways;[3] neither does His timing often match ours. I learned this in a dream, the only one I've ever had in which I knew while in the dream that I was face-to-face with Jesus:

> Jesus and I were in the kitchen area of a cruise ship. He was dressed as a Hibachi chef and was juggling sharp knives with as little concern as if they had been little rubber balls. We were having so much fun, both of us laughing hysterically; I remarked, "It's a good thing You're God or else You'd really hurt yourself!"
>
> On a café table was a collection of various seafoods, including a calamari steak. Jesus motioned me over and showed me how to cut it, handed me a knife, and said to slice off two or three pieces. I expected it to be tough and difficult to cut but it was as easy as going through soft butter. I was thrilled with what a great job I was doing so, chop-chop-chop, and it was done—a whole steak in about ten perfect slices—but then I looked up and Jesus' was walking away. "Come back, come back," I cried; and woke up.

Immediately, I knew that I'd gotten in a hurry because it seemed so easy, and had done more than He'd asked. A quick prayer of repentance and an attempt to go back to sleep and hopefully re-enter the dream was to no avail, but the lesson was learned. As the years have gone by, He has proven time and again that waiting on Him for both direction and timing is so much more effective than doing things my way. He is my best offensive weapon!

> *"Therefore wait for me," declares the Lord, "for the day when I rise up to seize the prey. For my decision is to gather nations, to assemble kingdoms, to pour out upon them my indignation, all my burning anger; for in the fire of my jealousy all the earth shall be consumed* [4]
>
> *Our soul waits for the Lord; he is our help and our shield.* [5]
>
> *...but they who wait for the Lord shall renew their strength; they shall mount up with wings like eagles; they shall run and not be weary; they shall walk and not faint.* [6]

Indeed, none who wait for you shall be put to shame; they shall be ashamed who are wantonly treacherous.[7]

Wait for the Lord; be strong, and let your heart take courage; wait for the Lord![8]

Wait for the Lord and keep his way, and he will exalt you to inherit the land; you will look on when the wicked are cut off.[9]

Do not say, "I will repay evil"; wait for the Lord, and he will deliver you.[10]

Granted, waiting doesn't come easy for most of us; we live in a time of instant gratification when just about anything we want or need can be obtained quickly via a quick order on the closest phone or computer. But while a drive-thru or microwave mentality can be helpful in everyday life, it's just not the way God usually operates and we need to change our focus to watch and see what the Father is doing before rushing into battle. After all, that's the way Jesus operated:

So Jesus said to them, "Truly, truly, I say to you, the Son can do nothing of his own accord, but only what he sees the Father doing. For whatever the Father does, that the Son does likewise.[11]

In the face of a difficult issue, we would do well to remember the account in 2 Chronicles 20 of King Jehoshaphat and the kingdom of Judah. A great multitude of warriors was approaching and both king and country were very afraid, but in wisdom they sought help from the Lord and He came through for them:

And the Spirit of the Lord came upon Jahaziel the son of Zechariah, son of Benaiah, son of Jeiel, son of Mattaniah, a Levite of the sons of Asaph, in the midst of the assembly. And he said, "Listen, all Judah and inhabitants of Jerusalem and King Jehoshaphat: Thus says the Lord to you, 'Do not be afraid and do not be dismayed at this great horde, for the battle is not yours but God's. Tomorrow go down against them. Behold, they will come up by the ascent of Ziz. You will find them at the end of the valley, east of the wilderness of Jeruel. You will not need to fight in this battle.

Stand firm, hold your position, and see the salvation of the Lord on your behalf, O Judah and Jerusalem.' Do not be afraid and do not be dismayed. Tomorrow go out against them, and the Lord will be with you." [12]

If we will only wait on the Lord, trust His word and be patient, He will do the same for us when the conflict seems overwhelming.

---

[1] John 17:16

[2] https://www.dictionary.com/e/pop-culture/hurry-up-and-wait/

[3] Isaiah 55:8

[4] Zephaniah 3:8

[5] Psalm 33:20

[6] Isaiah 40:31

[7] Psalm 25:3

[8] Psalm 27:14

[9] Psalm 37:34

[10] Proverbs 20:22

[11] John 5:19

[12] 2 Chronicles 20:14-17

CHAPTER FOUR

WHO AM I?

Who am I? It's a good question, and probably one each of us have often pondered. Oh, we may think we know, and are ready to toss out a verbal resume when asked to introduce ourselves, usually defining our identity by how we see ourselves. However, that view all-too-often boils down to our primary role(s) as spouse, parent or child, employer or employee, student or retiree, etc.; or it may revolve around the condition(s) in which we exist (i.e., chronical illness or physical fitness, wealth or poverty, brilliance or illiteracy, etc.); but there's a big difference between our true identity and all of that. Like an actor on a stage, a role is a part that we play and the set decorations are the conditions in which we play that role. Whenever our awareness of self is constricted to the manner in which we operate within our surroundings, we set ourselves up for less than the best God wants for us.

Think about the true source of your identity: If it comes from your job and you get fired, who are you? If it comes from your child and he grows up and flies away on his own, who are you? If it comes from your ability to excel at a particular skill or to compete and win at something, what happens if you can't do that anymore?

It gets worse, because identity goes far beyond the physical reality that is seen; it goes to straight to our hearts, where we have often nourished seeds of deception that convince us that we are worthless, inept, dumb, foolish, crazy, ugly, sinful, etcetera, etcetera, etcetera:

> *The heart is deceitful above all things, and desperately sick; who can understand it?[1]*

So what's the answer? Healthy hearts, and an ability to see ourselves as God sees us. Oh, that does sound good, but it also sounds like a pretty simplistic answer to a very difficult question.

How does one do that anyway? While we may understand God's desires for us in our heads, somehow our hearts haven't gotten the message; we still hurt, and all those tall weeds that have grown from such tiny seeds of deception can be very difficult to eradicate. Often, generational and/or inner-healing prayer is helpful, but the first step is to ponder and pray over what the Bible says because owning God's truth will set you free:[2]

> *For all who are led by the Spirit of God are sons of God. For you did not receive the spirit of slavery to fall back into fear, but you have received the Spirit of adoption as sons, by whom we cry, "Abba! Father!" The Spirit himself bears witness with our spirit that we are children of God, and if children, then heirs—heirs of God and fellow heirs with Christ, provided we suffer with him in order that we may also be glorified with him.[3]*

Some years back, I (Barbara) was driving along with my brother, Ross; his sixteen-year-old son was in the backseat, totally tuned into a video game on his phone—or so we thought. As we talked, something was said about Ross having adopted his first wife's eldest daughter, and suddenly Jadon's astonished voice erupted from behind, "What??? Jamie's adopted? How can she be adopted? You never told me that!!!" Now it was our turn to be surprised because it'd never been a secret and we just assumed everyone knew. But you see, my niece is so much a part of our family that any thought, let alone discussion, about adoption hardly ever comes up. In no way have her dad or grandparents or anyone else in the family ever seen her any differently than her half-siblings. Neither does God ever consider us to be anything less than His rightful children because we have been adopted into His family; we have been grafted in through the sacrifice of His only begotten Son, Jesus. The core of our true identity is that as Christians, we are God's kids and are legitimate heirs to His kingdom.

Identity is very much about knowing to whom you belong. In an earthly sense, another example is the story of an Argentinian man named Francisco Madariaga, whose pregnant mother, a doctor, was kidnapped and thrown into an Argentinean prison. He was born in the prison, stolen at birth, and taken home by a prison guard as a gift to his wife; but the home was filled with violence and abuse, and the boy never felt like he belonged. His birth mother simply disappeared, never to be seen again; but his birth father, who had fled into exile to avoid the same fate as his wife, never stopped looking for his son. Finally reunited with his real father after twenty-eight years, Francisco only stopped smiling when someone mentioned the name he had been given by the man who raised him. "Never again will I use that name," he said. "To have your identity is the most beautiful thing there is."[4]

Indeed, names are important, as is evident throughout scripture where the Lord changed names to reflect what one had become, or when He instructed parents what to name their children because of the prophetic meanings. Ultimately, we are so precious to Him that we will also receive new names:

> He who has an ear, let him hear what the Spirit says to the churches. To the one who conquers I will give some of the hidden manna, and I will give him a white stone, with a new name written on the stone that no one knows except the one who receives it.[5]

Do we understand how incredibly special such a new name is, a name known only by the Lord and the recipient? Such a name speaks to an intimacy with God that surpasses anything we experience on earth. When we don't comprehend our identity as a new creation in Christ, as a much-loved child of the King, we also have little idea of the power and authority that is available through Him; we are neither equipped to stand firm in faith or to forge ahead in the battle.

> Therefore, if anyone is in Christ, he is a new creation. The old has passed away; behold, the new has come.[6]

It is critical that we own our position in Jesus in order to understand and appropriate God's promises, which will enable us to engage and do serious damage to the enemy. God's truths empower us to persevere and overcome, because the enemy simply cannot stand in the face of God's truth, which is spiritually discerned:

The natural person does not accept the things of the Spirit of God, for they are folly to him, and he is not able to understand them because they are spiritually discerned. The spiritual person judges all things, but is himself to be judged by no one. "For who has understood the mind of the Lord so as to instruct him?" But we have the mind of Christ.[7]

Like Timothy, we are called to be soldiers of the cross:

Share in suffering as a good soldier of Christ Jesus. No soldier gets entangled in civilian pursuits, since his aim is to please the one who enlisted him.[8]

Soldiers are members of a military force, and any military develops both defensive and offensive tactics. It seems to me that the Church has been in a defensive posture for way too long and it's time to go on offense! We don't have to go it alone, so how can we lose?

I will not leave you as orphans; I will come to you... But the Helper, the Holy Spirit, whom the Father will send in my name, he will teach you all things and bring to your remembrance all that I have said to you. Peace I leave with you; my peace I give to you. Not as the world gives do I give to you. Let not your hearts be troubled, neither let them be afraid.[9]

Got that? *Let not your heart be troubled, neither let it be afraid.* As an adopted heir to the Kingdom of God, put on your armor and join the fight; take heart, for the enemy's battle strategy to divide and conquer is doomed to fail.

---

[1] Jeremiah 17:9 ESV

[2] John 8:32

[3] Romans 8:14-17 ESV

[4] https://www.sandiegouniontribune.com/sdut-argentine-stolen-at-birth-now-32-learns-identity-2010feb23-story.html

[5] Revelation 2:17 ESV

[6] 2 Corinthians 5:17

[7] 1 Corinthians 2:14-16
[8] 2 Timothy 2:3-4
[9] John 14:18, 26-27

CHAPTER FIVE

THE PART IS NOT THE WHOLE
PART 1

It seems that we are on a journey of discovery with the Lord in which He takes us back to re-visit things we've previously thought we understood. Apparently, those first exposures were simply foundational to greater levels of revelation; and so it is with the idea of 'the part is not the whole'. The Lord recently impressed me (Paul) to write about it, so I was shocked after-the-fact to learn that it was not only the subject but also the title of our first chapter in *Exploring Heavenly Places,* and the concept pops up here and there in other portions of that and other books as well. So, this 'new' article has been re-worked to incorporate what we now know into one place, though the Lord will undoubtedly continue to build upon our understanding. In keeping with the battle theme of this book, the concept of 'the part is not the whole' shines God's light into the darkness of another of the enemy's greatest weapons, divisiveness.

It is often a thought that establishes a wonderful principle in my mind, a thought that seems so simple at first that I am tempted just to forget it as a meaningless intrusion. However, as I am nudged by the Lord to seriously consider the ramifications of that thought, the enormity of the implications can astound me. In such a way, my consciousness was invaded one day in the midst of life's daily routines by the thought, "The part is not the whole." What in the world did it mean? How could such a random thought be as significant as this one seemed? I was unable to ignore or forget it, and 'the part is not whole' surfaced again and again, as if my mind was a computer processing a byte of necessary information to solve a complex mathematical equation.

'The part is not the whole' is historically rooted in my journey into prayer ministry, which began on October 7, 1989; in fact, you could say my life was simply routine until this day. A lady who wanted prayer for deliverance had called a few days earlier and we'd made an appointment, even though I had never prayed for someone in this way as a Baptist pastor. As I performed my first deliverance without knowing what I was doing, the Lord marvelously set her free and my prayer ministry journey began. This first session was a life-changing day and it became the basis of my first book, *Ravens: Unseen Evil, Unwilling Eyes*. My life has never been the same since, but this was just the first life-changing experience; there was much more to come.

A few months later, a man who had suffered severe childhood abuse approached me indicating that he needed help, and felt the Lord had directed him to me for prayer. I was not prepared for what happened next! Suddenly, I was not talking to the man but to a young boy expressing the pain he had tragically suffered as a victim of Satanic ritual abuse (SRA). This was my first experience with Multiple Personality Disorder (MPD), and following that session many others that had also experienced terrible pain as young children started coming for prayer. This was a psychological world that was both troubling and terrifying, and I was shocked at the reality of such evil. This was not something I had ever encountered in my twenty years as an American Baptist pastor who had grown up in a Southern Baptist church. This young man had been a member of the youth group many years before when I'd begun as a youth pastor; so the troubling question (both then and now) is how many other people that have endured such abuse have been right in front of us over the years, yet we never had a clue?

During our first appointment, the man shared that he had left the Baptist church to become part of a Vineyard congregation where he had grown in the prophetic. I began the prayer session, not at all prepared for what happened because suddenly his voice changed into that of a small boy. During the first few hours, other boy and girl voices spoke to me, and memories of unimaginable abuse were conveyed. We met several times over the next few months; I reeled from the horrific memories of extreme evil to which he was subjected, as well as ritualistic acts he was forced to participate in. Once, on vacation with my wife, Donna, I started tasting blood in my mouth. There was no apparent cause, but I wondered if it was somehow connected to the ministry with the young man so I called him and asked if he had done something. He replied, "I asked the Lord to let you taste blood if you really believe what has happened to me." My Baptist mind was blank! How could such a sensation happen? Physical discernment of spiritual manifestations has now become a way of life for me, but then it was completely foreign!

So began my prayer journey with people who had been diagnosed with MPD, now known as Dissociative Identity Disorder (DID). More and more people with this disorder began coming for prayer, and therapists who had worked in our church's counseling center started bringing their clients in as well.

One afternoon, a therapist brought in such a client, and we met in a Sunday school room on the west side of the church sanctuary. An intercessory team of three people had come to assist us, and as we prayed the Lord took the lady to a memory of abuse as a little girl. In the midst of her memory she turned to me and began speaking in a little girl's voice; but then she said in a completely different voice, "Paul, do you want to see her healed?" Internally, I really believed this was the Lord taking to me through her and I replied by saying, "Yes, Lord, I would like to see her totally healed." In those days I had all my prayers typed out because I didn't know what else to do, but the client started praying all them without any prompting on my part. I guess the Lord knew the prayers!

Then I felt the 'whoosh', a surge of power cascading from the top of my head to my feet. I turned to the others in the room and asked, "Did you feel that?" Everyone confirmed that they had felt the same sensation. For the first time in my life I understood the physical manifestation of the power of the Holy Spirit. Not only that, but the change in the client was startling, and she left a totally different person. The next day my secretary came in and commented, "Whatever happened in that room is still there." Walking into the room, I could feel a tingling sensation all over me, along with an awareness of God's power. I walked into the sanctuary and could feel what seemed like a river of that power flowing across the front of the sanctuary.

The Lord continued teaching me systematically about ministering to people with DID, but I've come to realize today that methods and models of ministry are not enough. We must welcome the aggressive power of the Holy Spirit as He moves within the DID system of a person in order to see results that are long lasting. Back then, even as I continued to pastor and minister through prayer, I started having an uneasy feeling that I was to discontinue my work with DID sufferers. I was now pastoring another church, and many with DID were still coming for prayer; but despite the pressure from these hurting people seeking help, the Lord told me to stop working with them. I was mystified, and second-guessed my decision to quit; but in retrospect it's clear that the Lord wanted to bring me back into balance, and to have a healthy perspective when dealing with DID that is a result of catastrophic abuse.

Within a couple of years, The Lord released me to minister to these gifted and wounded people once again; but in the meantime, I listened to every recording I could find about DID and devoured every book I could read that explained this defense mechanism of our body, soul and spirit.

In 1994 the American Psychiatric Association, in its publication of the *Diagnostic and Statistical Manual of Mental Disorders* (DSM-IV), the term 'Multiple Dissociative Disorder' was changed to 'Dissociative Identity Disorder' (DID) in order to more accurately describe the malady.[1] Since those early years, extensive research both by Christians and the academic community has explored the staggering complexities of DID.

In 1998, a mutual friend introduced me to Dr. Tom Hawkins, who had also previously been exposed to DID. He had come to our home for a seven-day visit when we were living on the property of the Center for Prayer Mobilization in Idyllwild CA, and a wonderful friendship developed. We later spent much more time together and often talked by phone as we matured in our understanding about DID. Tom's ministry, Restoration in Christ Ministries, became a leader in helping those who were severely abused by others.[2]

A person with DID can have many parts, often known as alter identities or alters, and Dr. Tom Hawkins has given us a good definition of an alter:

> An alter-identity is a completely separated projection of the person's true self, formed through dissociation to enable him to cope in the midst of overwhelming trauma. This is a more accurate designation than alter-personality, as each of these parts has a distinct identity but not always a completely developed personality. They are much more limited in function and awareness than primary identities, which carry the strongest essence of self.[3]

Many years of ministry and study has taught me that the diagnosis of DID can be seen as many different levels of dissociation. A person can experience a simple dissociation, such as being at the dentist and escaping in your mind to a pleasant place like a park; you don't want to be in the chair, you do want to avoid the pain of the moment, and your mind can escape by going somewhere pleasant. We can also dissociate when we are driving long distances and suddenly find ourselves at the needed offramp, wondering how we got to that point; but dissociation from abuse goes a lot deeper. As the level of abuse increases, the intense pain can result in parts being developed; whole personalities are formed and become isolated in order to serve many different functions. These parts can be hidden from the main, or host, personality so that the person is unaware of them until an event triggers something that allows the parts to come to the surface of the person's psyche. In fact, as I have talked to parts, they often exhibit the characteristics of the person, sometimes thinking they are the only one in the body.

In ministering to the parts, we have learned that while a part can manifest as a complete individual and all aspects of a total person can be seen in the part, there are also times when the part believes that he or she is the entire person. For example, a three-year-old part may have the memories and personality of a three-year-old; he is everything that a three-year-old is, yet it is only a part; it is not the entire self. This separation from the core identity allows the parts of the whole person to be scattered, and relegated to different places in the spiritual world. Each part has the appearance of the whole, and might even function as a whole; but it is only a part; and each part can hold unpleasant memories from the past; but again, the part is not the whole person. The concept of DNA provides a good illustration: each cell contains the complex information of the entire person, but that small part is not the whole individual; it is only a part, and a microscopic one at that.

During the ministry of inner healing, these deep-seated wounds can be discovered through the guidance of the Holy Spirit, and healing can occur. The process of acknowledging the memory, the part, and allowing it to be brought back into the whole of a person is called integration. This may be as simple as remembering an unkind word that caused us to be stuck in the past and is quickly resolved. Or, it may be the result of one or many horrific experience(s) that caused a part to be totally isolated from all other parts, in which case the process of integration may be a complex process of many steps. These steps may include remembering an event, acknowledging the memory, forgiving those who caused the injury, and perhaps even forgiving oneself or forgiving God.

---

[1] http://www.rcm-usa.org/ *Dissociative Identity Disorder: Recognizing and Restoring the Severely Abused* Tom R. Hawkins, Ph.D. "Dissociation is generally considered to be a disturbance or alteration in consciousness, memory, identity or perception of the environment. Normally, a person integrates these various functions, whereas dissociation is a compartmentalization of these functions. Dissociation is a process whereby the mind separates one or more aspects of its function (knowing, feeling, tasting, hearing, seeing, etc.) away from the normal stream of consciousness. Dissociation lies on a continuum ranging from the normal phenomena of day dreaming, fantasy, and "highway hypnosis" on the one end to the poly-fragmented (highly complex) multiple whose mind is split into hundreds (or thousands) of separate identities on the other end. This condition was formerly known as Multiple Personality Disorder (MPD), but was changed to Dissociative Identity Disorder (DID) in 1994 by the American Psychiatric Association with its publication of DSM-IV, in order to more accurately describe the disorder."

[2] Tom Hawkins passed away a few years ago and Diane Hawkins how

leads Restoration in Christ Ministries.

[3]http://www.rcm-usa.org/ *Dissociative Identity Disorder: Recognizing and Restoring the Severely Abused*. Tom R. Hawkins, Ph.D.

CHAPTER SIX

THE PART IS NOT THE WHOLE

PART 2

In the fall of 2017, Donna and I ministered for five Sundays at Mountain View Community Church in Kaneohe, Hawaii. Each Sunday was an adventure in preaching; the Lord would instruct me, sometimes at the last minute, on the subject I was to speak about. One morning I woke up and heard the word 'complete'. I made every attempt to go back to sleep but it was impossible. 'Complete' was ricocheting between different places in my mind, and sleep was now elusive so I struggled out of bed and sat in the chair.

Through dreary and sleep-deprived eyes, I booted up my computer and opened my Bible software wondering where the word 'complete' is found in scripture. I noticed Matthew 19:20-21:

> The young man said to Him, 'All these things I have kept from my youth. What do I still lack?' Jesus said to him, 'If you want to be perfect, go, sell what you have and give to the poor, and you will have treasure in heaven; and come, follow Me."

I wondered what the Greek definition of 'perfect' was, so I did a search and discovered that the 'perfect' actually means 'complete'. The same word is used in Colossians 1:28:

> "Him we preach, warning every man and teaching every man in all wisdom, that we may present every man perfect [complete] in Christ Jesus.

The Greek word for 'complete' is *teleios*, which means 'whole'; of sacrifices, 'without blemish'; with no part outside, nothing that belongs is left out of the soul and its full faculties. It is maturity. In

Greek philosophy it was the point of total humanity. It is the fellowship of families and localities in full and self-sufficient life, and this completeness leads to happiness. It is an unblemished, undivided, complete whole so the heart is undivided.[1]

I may have been tired and sleepy, but the Lord used that moment to show me that the goal in our life is to be 'complete' so that there are no parts left outside, but dissociated parts of an individual can be scattered into many places, both inside and outside of the body; places such as the ungodly width, length, depth and height,[2] the ungodly spiritual stars, star systems, constellations, zodiacs and galaxies, or places in time other than the present. What happens to them? Frankly, the complexities are beyond our understanding; but fortunately, God does understand and He wants to see us brought back into wholeness so that we can be all that He has made us to be.

I have often been troubled because I could not understand how a person could be trapped in so many different places at the same time. How could one function in life on earth and yet inhabit many other places in the spiritual world? Furthermore, as the soul or spirit is fractured into parts and scattered into various places, the obvious question is what happens to them there. As we experienced our own revelation, we noticed that many others were receiving similar truths. Ana Méndez Farrell writes in her book, *Regions of Captivity*, about ministering to her hospitalized sister. The Lord showed Ana that her sister was trapped in an underwater cave, and she provides a visual image of her vision in the book. The Lord revealed to Ana how to minster to her sister, and the result was a wonderful healing. I was astonished because I was already aware of how the Lord had shown many people through dreams and visions that they or others were also trapped under water. How was this possible? It was clear that Ana could see her sister in the hospital room, yet she also saw her under water. How could she be in two places at one time? It was while looking at Ana's picture that I had a sudden realization that 'the part is not the whole' finally made sense, and then I finally understood. 'The part is not the whole' wasn't such a random thought after all! It is a truth that has deeply affected me; it is a truth that has enhanced my understanding of the complexity of issues that affect the function of the human being. Even so, my mind still reels while trying to grasp the enormity of the implications of what can happen to one's body, soul, and spirit.

To add to the complexity of this reality, dissociation can happen in the generational line as well, and separated generational parts still seem to have influence on a person who is alive today. It is also possible that these parts have been fragmented so that the solution to finding a part and bringing it back to the body is only solved by first bringing the fragments back to the part, at which point the part can be addressed through the Lord's guidance in prayer, returned to the person, and placed into the Lord's perfect time.

Since such scattering has been the result of terrible wounding and the Lord can undo the work of the enemy, wholeness can be achieved. God is always greater! This is a truth that is well illustrated by the psalmist as he praises the Lord for delivering him from Sheol, which is located in the ungodly depth.[3] The psalmist expresses this concept in Psalm 86:11-13:

> *Teach me Your way, O LORD;*
> *I will walk in Your truth;*
> *Unite my heart to fear Your name.*
> *I will praise You, O Lord my God, with all my heart,*
> *And I will glorify Your name forevermore.*
> *For great is Your mercy toward me,*
> *And You have delivered my soul from the depths of Sheol.*

In this poetic expression, David is asking the Lord to unite his heart and to deliver him from Sheol. The word 'unite' is the Hebrew word *yahad,* which means 'unitedness', 'unit', 'together' and 'altogether'. It is interesting that the word is translated in the Septuagint as *homothumadon,* which means 'with one mind' or 'unanimously'.[4] The word is often used as a term of unity among believers, but is it possible that it also designates a personality that is no longer fractured, but unified or 'complete'?

The complexity of this is staggering, but everyday reality lends context to how common it is. It is not unusual to find that a person's tormented-and-separated parts relate to the exterior, physical world in ways that shock us. How often have you talked to someone and been astonished by their response to you? You might attribute what is happening to them as a bad mood, while in reality you are actually relating to a wounded part that is now responding to a comment from you. It is then compounded when, perhaps, a wounded part of you responds and the conversation spirals downward into a heated debate or fight. Then both of you walk away, confused by the reaction of the other, wondering what just happened in the midst of a seemingly civilized conversation, and asking, "What did I say wrong?"

While pondering all of this, I suddenly had a profound thought. We know Jesus is coming back for a complete bride, we know that He wants a Body that is in complete unity, and we have had endless discussions about the need for unity in the Body of Christ; but what if there is another layer of unity that we have not considered? What if we first need to have unity within our own bodies? Indeed, without unity within ourselves, we really cannot conceive of unity with others. Is 'oneness', or unity, even possible with others unless I am one within myself?

The strategy of the enemy is not only to keep us from achieving oneness with others, but also from experiencing unity within ourselves. The enemy scatters us so that he can steal that which God has given us, and then transform it into power to accomplish his own purposes. The enemy scatters us in ungodly heavenly places in woundedness, rejection, shame, loneliness, pain, fear and whatever else, so that we become unable to walk in or utilize the power and blessings that the Lord wants for our internal unity.

There is a very interesting passage in Genesis 11:6:

> And the LORD said, "Indeed the people are one and they all have one language, and this is what they begin to do; now nothing that they propose to do will be withheld from them."

The people at the tower of Babel were unified for evil purposes. They were building a tower to reach into the heavens (not heaven); in other words, they were building a tower to reach into the dimensions. These people were exercising a God-given principle of unity, which dictated that there would be success for *nothing that they purposed to do will be withheld from them.*

Let's take this a step further. What happens if the enemy scatters each individual person into many parts that now operate in unity within the person, not for God but for the enemy? The enemy operates within these parts, convincing them of the bad intentions of the Lord so they come into agreement (unity) to work on behalf of the enemy rather than the Lord. I have pondered if this is an aspect of the 'mystery of Babylon'. What if the enemy takes all of the scattered soul and spirit parts of humanity, and utilizes them in unity for the sole purpose of taking over the Kingdom of Heaven and the Kingdom of God in order to set up his own kingdom? We are now back to the beginning of Babylon/Tower of Babel, and the enemy's original intent to create unity for the purpose of dethroning God and establishing an evil empire. It's the same old scheme, just using a slightly different tactic.

Perhaps Deuteronomy 30:4-6 has a deeper meaning then we have imagined:

> *If any of you are driven out to the farthest parts under heaven, from there the LORD your God will gather you, and from there He will bring you. Then the LORD your God will bring you to the land which your fathers possessed, and you shall possess it. He will prosper you and multiply you more than your fathers. And the LORD your God will circumcise your heart and the heart of your descendants, to love the LORD your God with all your heart and with all your soul, that you may live.*

Notice Moses says, *with all your heart and with all your soul.* We must be one; we must be complete to do this! Is it even possible to fully love the Lord and to follow Him until we are one inside?

King David knew that he could actually be torn into pieces, and that he needed to be delivered from the enemy.

> O LORD *my God, in You I put my trust; Save me from all those who persecute me; And deliver me, Lest they tear me like a lion, Rending me in pieces, while there is none to deliver.*[5]

As I became more experienced in relating to the parts of people, I began asking if the part was inside or outside of the body. Very often, I would get a response that would surprise the client as a part would say, "I am outside of the body." I would then have follow-up questions. "What's it like where you are?" And they might say: "It's real cold"; "It's really empty"; "I'm in a void"; "I'm in a black hole"; or "I'm attached to a star". This condition is very painful for the parts, as well as for the person, and the internal conflict is the source of much suffering. Proverbs 18:14 reminds us:

> *The spirit of a man can endure sickness but as for a broken spirit who can bear it.*

As I was relating these insights to the people of Mountain View, a lady in the congregation raised a hand. I invited her to share and she said, "When I woke up this morning, I'd had a dream about outside line tables, and the glass was shattered like tempered glass that breaks into a million pieces. I was cleaning it up off the grass; there was shattered glass everywhere." Another person raised a hand and volunteered, "When she said that, I saw shattered glass all over the entire floor of the cafeteria."

Pastor Rob then shared the dream he had early that morning.

> I had a bizarre dream in which I kept going in and out of the dream; I would sleep great and wake up refreshed, but while in the dream I felt so disconnected. In the first scene I was in the back of a bus, dressed as a German soldier and there were German soldiers in front of me. I was aghast that one of the soldiers took a gun and shot a fellow soldier in the head, and then I'm like, "I'm out of here!" I started going down the middle isle but they all

pushed me to the back of the bus, and started shooting one another. I shared this with my wife and she said, "Oh, that's dis-unity in the church." Next, I found myself outside an elementary school, but not here; it's in the salt lake area of Honolulu. Pastor Jason was there and he helped me go into a door; and I saw Pastor Tisha, who also went into a door. There I was in the school, going down a long corridor through all these doors and as I went through each one, I made sure they were closed; I think the doors went into heavenly places. There was an enormous screen with a child's cartoon playing, and our worship service was about to start but I realized that our worship team wasn't there. I turned to Pastor Barb and asked, "Where's our worship team?" She answered, "There's no worship team here today Rob; they're not here." I asked, "How come they're not here?" She responded, "You never told them to come here." I was really frustrated, and then realized I didn't have my sermon notes. Thinking they were in my car, I went out to the parking lot, but now my car was not there; so, I'm just in total frustration, not connected at all. I noticed a friend and asked, "Why are you here?" He said, "I'm going surfing," but I'm thinking, "Dude, why? Nothing is united, everything is scattered, and I'm flustered." Then I got up and began sharing with a congregation of people that I didn't recognize; they seemed to be from different cities across the United States. I was explaining how our church flows and what's supposed to happen, while also apologizing that things were not going well. The people began getting up and leaving one by one. There was no unity. It was the most perplexing dream I've ever had. I hated it! It's clear now that I was feeling disunity, not of our congregation because we're a very united church, but the disunity within each of us, the parts of the person.

As I finished with the sermon, Rob interrupted me to share that he had just received a text from someone in the congregation saying that the previous day had been Armistice Day, the day of freedom in France. Armistice Day is commemorated every year on November 11th to mark the armistice, or peace agreement, signed between the Allies of WWI and Germany for ending the hostility. It took effect at 11 AM, on the 11th hour, of the 11th day, of the 11th month of 1918. I found this to be very profound, for the Lord wants to see an armistice among the scattered parts within a person, an end to the hostilities with one other, the person, and the Lord. His desire for us is for there to finally be peace.

So, what is the solution? In ministry, the Lord has shown us that He can rescue all these parts no matter where they are or how far away they are. Nehemiah 1:5-11 provides a startling, and illuminating, statement (notice another 11—the prayer ends on 1:11):

And I said: "I pray, LORD God of heaven, O great and awesome God, You who keep Your covenant and mercy with those who love You and observe Your commandments, please let Your ear be attentive and Your eyes open, that You may hear the prayer of Your servant which I pray before You now, day and night, for the children of Israel Your servants, and confess the sins of the children of Israel which we have sinned against You. Both my father's house and I have sinned. We have acted very corruptly against You, and have not kept the commandments, the statutes, nor the ordinances which You commanded Your servant Moses. Remember, I pray, the word that You commanded Your servant Moses, saying, 'If you are unfaithful, I will scatter you among the nations; but if you return to Me, and keep My commandments and do them, though some of you were cast out to the farthest part of the heavens, yet I will gather them from there, and bring them to the place which I have chosen as a dwelling for My name.' Now these are Your servants and Your people, whom You have redeemed by Your great power, and by Your strong hand. O Lord, I pray, please let Your ear be attentive to the prayer of Your servant, and to the prayer of Your servants who desire to fear Your name; and let Your servant prosper this day, I pray, and grant him mercy in the sight of this man." [6]

Though it may be that you will want to have someone else help you with pursuing your integration, the Lord has given a prayer as a beginning step for rescuing our scattered parts:

> Father, please rescue me from every ungodly place to which I've been scattered in my lifetime and make me complete. Please retrieve every part of me that is entrapped in the ungodly width, length, depth and height, time, the stars, the zodiac or on the ungodly grid. Please disconnect me from all ungodly spiritual beings and return to me through Your blood every shattered part of my soul and spirit. Lord, I desperately desire to have an undivided heart so that I may be united with myself, united with others, and united with You. In Jesus name, I now give each of my scattered parts permission to feel and express all the emotions bottled up inside of me. Father, please send the chariots of fire to rescue all scattered parts; please release the Lion of Judah to release the sound that will bring integration and unification. Amen.

---

[1] Delling, G. (1964–). τέλος, τελέω, ἐπιτελέω, συντελέω, συντέλεια, παντελής, τέλειος, τελειότης, τελειόω, τελείωσις, τελειωτής. G. Kittel, G. W. Bromiley, & G. Friedrich (Eds.), *Theological dictionary of the New Testament* (electronic ed., Vol. 8, p. 67). Grand Rapids, MI: Eerdmans.

[2] For more information, see *Exploring Heavenly Places, Volume 9: Travel Guide to the Width, Length, Depth and Height*

[3] See *Exploring Heavenly Places, Volume 1* for more information regarding locations in and effects of the ungodly depth, as well as *The Prayer to Release One From the Ungodly Depth*, which is also available at http://aslansplace.com/language/en/prayer-to-release-one-from-the-ungodly-depth/

[4] Gilchrist, P. R. (1999). 858 יָחַד. R. L. Harris, G. L. Archer Jr., & B. K. Waltke (Eds.), *Theological Wordbook of the Old Testament* (electronic ed., p. 373). Chicago: Moody Press.

[5] Psalm 7:1-2.

[6] See also Deuteronomy 30:4 and Isaiah 41:8

CHAPTER SEVEN

UNITY WITHIN THE CHURCH

When I (Barbara) was a teenager, our church was building a new sanctuary/office/educational wing. My mother was on the building committee and as she attended one of the meetings, I waited in the car so I could get in some practice driving time. After a while Mom came storming out, got in the car and slammed the door, so angry she was seeing red. Red carpets, that is! And she didn't want red; she wanted blue, which is what we finally ended up with if I recall correctly. My point is, that committee meeting was by no means a picture of the Body coming together in unity, and most Christians who've grown up in churches of any denomination probably could tell similar stories. And, don't even get me started on the actual all-church business meetings!

We have to wonder; we have to ask, "Is unity within the Church even possible?" And of course, the answer is yes because God never advises us to accomplish that which is impossible:

> *Behold, how good and pleasant it is when brothers dwell in unity!* [1]

> *The glory that you have given me I have given to them, that they may be one even as we are one, I in them and you in me, that they may become perfectly one, so that the world may know that you sent me and loved them even as you loved me.* [2]

> *Live in harmony with one another.* [3]

Apostle Paul's familiar advice to the Corinthians used the physical body as an accurate picture of how the Church Body is supposed to function. [4] Have you ever stubbed your big toe, had a headache, or cut your finger? Of course you have, and so have I; each of us is well aware that each isolated injury, no matter how seemingly insignificant, immediately takes the center stage of our attention. Worse, if one suffers from a major illness such as cancer or heart disease, the whole body quickly engages in the suffering; everything hurts, strength flees, and often hopelessness and fear set in on top of everything else. As it is with the physical body, so it is in the Church; no one person is more important than another and it takes everyone functioning according to their specific spiritual gifts to become and remain effective.

I have been incredibly blessed by God to have had the privilege to come alongside the ministry of Aslan's Place since January 2005. It is here that I have, for the first time in my life, experienced unity within the Body on a consistent basis. There are a number of reasons for this, first and foremost being that everyone pretty-much checks their own agendas and pet doctrines at the door in order to strictly follow the lead of the Holy Spirit. Additionally, the Bible is the final test of truth regarding everything that is said or done; and each person is valued as a necessary part of the group where the practice and use of individual spiritual gifts is encouraged. Meeting guidelines,[5] developed by Brian Cox,[6] are also very helpful.

That sounds nice, but what does it look like? What are the results? A few examples might be helpful, and the first that comes to mind is the way the generational prayers have been developed. Most people can probably relate more to my mom's building committee experience where disagreements reigned than they can to groups (ranging from just a few to over fifty) writing one prayer with no dissent; let alone the many that are included in the current version of *Generational Prayers,* which exceeds 200 pages. How did that happen? We followed the Spirit; we carefully recorded and heeded messages from the Lord; we listened to and considered what everyone had to say; we prayed the new prayers in their rough format and later edited them for publication; and with every prayer, we have seen both individual and personal breakthroughs.

In 2018, the Lord led Paul to begin what came to be known as the Healing Well. A small group of us met to discuss what this would look like and through a bit of trial and error, refined the program into a workable format. The concept is that we come together as a larger group to prep for the day, breaking down into small groups of about 4-6 people to pray for individuals who have requested prayer. Each appointment is only 40 minutes. At the end the day, we come back together to debrief, share testimonies of what God taught us and/or accomplished through us. Depending on the number of teams, we often pray for 20-30 people at each Healing Well event. Our goal is to equip Christians to become comfortable enough to begin praying for others routinely in their daily lives, having had the opportunity to learn to do so in a safe teaching environment.

A testimony from a lady who attended the Aslan's Place Academy in March 2019, provides a comprehensive look at how God orchestrated events to utilize the unity of the Body to deliver healing to His daughter. Usually, the academies fill up months in advance, but this one was unusual in that several people were prompted to register at the last minute, this woman being one of them. She both received individual prayer from a couple of prayer ministers early in the week and was also one of the people chosen to receive prayer during a Healing Well on Thursday. It had quickly become obvious to many that she was struggling, and though she was unaware of it at that time, most attendees were praying for her. Excerpts of her testimony clearly show how God orchestrated events and used the various spiritual gifts of a number of people to bring forth new levels of freedom:

> Aslan's Place is decorated with beautiful art pieces, with many expressing the theme of the Lion of Judah; and Jana Green,[7] a wonderful prophetic artist, happened to showcase her paintings in one of the rooms. When I saw them, my spirit was so filled with joy that I was literally jolted physically. Two paintings especially rocked me; one with white horses galloping with long flowing manes[8] and the other with Jesus' hands cupping His living water, which dripped down into a body of water.[9]
>
> Jana explained that the horses depicted the events of 2 Samuel 5:20. David had inquired of the Lord and defeated the Philistines as God had promised; he named the place 'Baal-Perazim', which means, "The Lord has broken

through my enemies before me like a breaking flood". My spirit was moved, and my body turned and yelled, "Wooh!" because I remembered praying about that last year.

By God's grace, I was selected to receive prayer during a Healing Well session. As soon as I sat down, the team facilitator, who is a seer, discerned that the lady taking notes had a word of knowledge for me. The lady looked puzzled, so I presumed she didn't have anything yet.

Everyone on the team participated; one got a picture, one had a word of knowledge, another was praying, one was worshipping, and another was taking notes while the facilitator followed the Spirit's lead to direct the session. Someone saw an ungodly lion spirit and called it out. They were all praying for me for what felt like thirty minutes or longer.

Things changed when one of the veteran prayer ministers walked into the room; somehow I felt encouraged because there was another person to help. I mentally decided that I needed to take more authority and fight this false lion spirit, though I was very tired by that point and felt like I didn't have much breath. I tried to say, "In Jesus name, stop tormenting me". However, what came out of my mouth was a very weak complaint, "Jesus is tormenting me". I was told later by one of the ladies that those words encouraged the team to fight even harder against this false lion spirit.

Then the facilitator saw an angel and asked the Lord's permission to call on the help of that angel; thankfully, permission was granted by Holy Spirit. She saw the angel standing near her and asked me to walk through the area where it stood. I managed to stumble across the room and fell on my knees at the spot where the angel was located; then I walked on my knees through the spot and she started exclaiming, "It's a gate! It's the floodgates! It's the floodgates!".

The facilitator then realized that the lady whom she felt had a word of knowledge for me at the beginning was to give me her word, which was to roar over me. At the sound of her roaring, the false lion left and those in the room discerned it going.

I then fell into the prayer minister's arms, crying with immense gratitude, marvelling at the Lord, at the Body of Christ, and at His amazing love.

The Lord chose six ladies and angels on assignment to fight with me against this generational false lion; and I knew this could only have taken place at the REAL Lion's place—at Aslan's Place!!! When I shared my testimony briefly at the end of the Academy, Paul Cox said 1 Corinthians 14 took place during my session. AMEN, and all glory to HIM!

Later, as I reminisced about what the Lord had done for me, I realized that He had broken through my enemies before me like a breaking flood when I crossed through the floodgates in His Presence with angelic help. The Lord opened the floodgates to save me; He'd tried to tell me earlier with Jana's paintings, but I didn't get it then. Hallelujah!!!

So you see, unity in the Body, as illustrated in 1 Corinthians 14, is possible in the world today! As time passes, we are beginning to hear more and more testimonies of astounding moves of God in people's lives when Christians, not only at Aslan's Place but also in other gatherings, come together in unity to celebrate Him. How exciting it is to live in this time when we are privileged watch the Lion of Judah on the move. Even, so, Lord Jesus, come!

---

[1] Psalm 133:1

[2] John 17:22-23

[3] Romans 12:16

[4] 1 Corinthians 12:12-31

[5] Meeting Guidelines are available at
http://aslansplace.com/language/en/about-us/meeting-guidelines/

[6] Brian Cox, Paul's son, is an integral part of Aslan's Place; in addition to a myriad of other responsibilities, he is a brilliant teacher, a gifted prayer minister and the developer of the website

[7] Jana Green is a prayer minister, as well as a gifted artist who contributed the drawings in *Exploring Heavenly Places, Volume 7: Discernment Encyclopedia for God's Spiritual Creation*. Her website is
http://www.signsandwondersstudio.com

[8] Baal-Perazim can be viewed and/or purchased on Jana's website at
https://www.signsandwondersstudio.com/shop/baal-perazim

[9] The Pouring Out can be viewed and/or purchased on Jana's website at
https://www.signsandwondersstudio.com/shop/the-pouring-out

CHAPTER EIGHT
LEGAL REMEDIES

Popular culture, or pop culture as it is commonly known, generally refers to the practices, beliefs and objects that are dominant, or even ubiquitous, in a society or group at a given point in time.[1] Over the years, Christianity has experienced its own episodes of biblical pop culture as particular teachings or beliefs have become acclaimed by large numbers of people, sometimes for better and some for worse. Some of these fads, for lack of a better word, often have had great biblical beginnings, but at some point have moved a bit off the mark, which is dangerous in the righteous spiritual arena.

Currently popular is the idea of running off to a heavenly court with every prayer request, and there's no doubt that it is sometimes a great idea, but—and it's a big BUT—we should never be doing it unless we discern that is where the Holy Spirit is taking us. While the heavenly courts present a wonderful legal remedy, they are not an all-encompassing solution to every skirmish in the war. If it was Jesus' own practice to discern before doing, it certainly should be ours as well, and:

> *So Jesus said to them, "Truly, truly, I say to you, the Son can do nothing of his own accord, but only what he sees the Father doing. For whatever the Father does, that the Son does likewise.*[2]

Most assuredly, there are times when entering God's heavenly courts is appropriate, and may indeed be the venue in which the Lord prefers to wage war on our behalf. He first began bringing us there in 2005, and those initial experiences regarding how that came about have already been written.[3] Since that time, we've experienced some astounding deliverance in heavenly courts, some of which we'll share; but first, a few biblical references:

If he passes through and imprisons and summons the court, who can turn him back? [4]

He calls to the heavens above and to the earth, that he may judge his people: "Gather to me my faithful ones, who made a covenant with me by sacrifice! The heavens declare his righteousness, for God himself is judge!" [5]

For out of Zion shall go forth the law, and the word of the Lord from Jerusalem. He shall judge between the nations, and shall decide disputes for many peoples; and they shall beat their swords into plowshares, and their spears into pruning hooks; nation shall not lift up sword against nation, neither shall they learn war anymore. [6]

For the Lord is our judge; the Lord is our lawgiver; the Lord is our king; he will save us. [7]

But you have come to Mount Zion and to the city of the living God, the heavenly Jerusalem, and to innumerable angels in festal gathering, and to the assembly of the firstborn who are enrolled in heaven, and to God, the judge of all, and to the spirits of the righteous made perfect... [8]

In the future there is laid up for me the crown of righteousness, which the Lord, the righteous Judge, will award to me on that day; and not only to me, but also to all who have loved His appearing...There is only one Lawgiver and Judge, the One who is able to save and to destroy; but who are you who judge your neighbor? [9]

As the Lord, the righteous Judge, has ushered us into His courts over the years, we have often found ourselves in the Ancient of Days Court, which Daniel experienced many long centuries before we did:

In the first year of Belshazzar king of Babylon, Daniel saw a dream and visions of his head as he lay in his bed... "As I looked, thrones were placed, and the Ancient of Days took his seat; his clothing was white as snow, and the hair of his head like pure wool; his throne was fiery flames; its wheels were burning fire. A stream of fire issued and came out from before him;

a thousand thousands served him, and ten thousand times ten thousand stood before him; the court sat in judgment, and the books were opened…"I saw in the night visions, and behold, with the clouds of heaven there came one like a son of man, and he came to the Ancient of Days and was presented before him. And to him was given dominion and glory and a kingdom, that all peoples, nations, and languages should serve him; his dominion is an everlasting dominion, which shall not pass away, and his kingdom one that shall not be destroyed.[10]

Needless to say, this is not a court that should be taken lightly; it is a court where the Ancient of Days addresses matters of tremendous importance. In 2014, a leadership summit at Aslan's Place was the setting for one such occasion. Larry Pearson[11] was speaking:

I acknowledge the Ancient of Days, I acknowledge that I do not stand in my name, my strength or anything of me, or anything of humanity; I acknowledge the Name Above All Names and the Ancient of Days, Who gave authority to man to set up thrones. We are in the counsel of the Lord, not the counsel of man but the counsel of the Lord. I seek the sound of the Ancient of Days, I acknowledge the sound of the Ancient of Days…I acknowledge [His] eternal power and majesty and glory; I acknowledge Christ the prophet and apostle, and I acknowledge His work; I acknowledge His power of an endless life; I acknowledge who He is as He is, not who He was but who He is, the wounded who ascended, the Chief of Chiefs, the Cornerstone alone. He is the Lord of Lords, the King of Kings and the One who summons the kings, Who binds the kings, Who destroyed the king of lies. The king of lies has been defeated, he's been defeated, he's been defeated!

Father, I acknowledge the office that has been bestowed upon me because of your call, because of your word, and because of your purpose; I come to Most High God, the righteous Judge of heaven and earth, and I petition this high court to release this decree of a higher light to expose, to expose, to expose; and to divide asunder. All the disguises will fall, all the disguises will fall. I ask for a decree for the path of de-masking, the de-masking of the false church (the Lion roars); the de-masking of the false church, of the hierarchy, the de-masking and removal of the mixture that You, King of Glory, may come without measure. I petition the court based on the shed blood of Jesus Christ, to serve notice for the one (Satan), that has locked and made hidden the north gate that he has covered over, and has hidden and buried the glory that is ours as sons and daughters of the Most High God. He has buried and covered over the ancient gate and the ancient path. I petition the high court to execute the will of the King, to release the holy fire of God, to tear down the systems of the father of lies. May this be the hour and the time when the clocks change back to Kairos, and a North American time change be released. May there be a synchronicity so that the north gate will be opened and the enemy displaced, and an alignment for the kings from the King of Glory to find their place, find their time, and be triangulated in their royal crowning of the greater glory.

The whirlwinds are coming; the whirlwinds are coming from the north. The greater strength of the angelic host is coming from heaven, as whirlwinds from the north, to execute the judgment of the King so that the river of God will flow wheresoever it will be decreed before the foundations.

You are in My time; you are in My space; I love it when you get in My space. Come up, My beloved, come up into My space and see My face.

The government is rising; the future government is rising. Fire is coming; the fire is coming; He is coming in the clouds; He is coming in the clouds; He is coming in the clouds. He is making a sound; He is living out loud through you and me. True liberty; you will find My rhythm in the glory; you will find My rhythm in the glory. Awaken, awaken, awaken; do you feel the rhythm of My glory? He's coming in the clouds, with power and thunder and lightning... Look up! A wave is coming... It's going to touch every mountain, and awaken a tsunami to the uttermost parts of the earth.

All in attendance were in awe of what we were experiencing, and Paul responded to Larry's word, "While you were prophesying, I saw two lightning strikes hit Satan, and I feel like tentacles are coming off of us."

An entire book would be required to adequately recount even a fraction of our courtroom experiences, but our intent here is only to illustrate that heavenly court appearances are very much a part of the spiritual battle in which we are engaged. Our physical reality often reflects a much larger spiritual reality, and the physical court system is no exception. On earth, we don't have one-size-fits-all courts—in the USA, they vary from small claims or traffic courts to the US Supreme Court. If for no other reason than the vast expanses of the unseen dimensions, the heavenly court system far exceeds anything we can know here; but a few courts we have experienced in addition to the Ancient of Days Court include:

- Mount Zion Court (which we think is the highest court)
- Bankruptcy Court
- Family Court
- Supreme Court
- World Court
- Melchizedek Court
- A court to change frequencies
- Court of Grievances
- Time Court

It's clear that the enemy is a legalist who is always searching for loopholes, for new legal rights to come against us; hitting us upside the head with guilt over infractions of God's laws. Meanwhile, he's also desperately trying to deflect the truth of God's grace and mercy, keeping us as far away as possible from His forgiveness and redemption, which truly are freely available. A legal remedy is what is required; fortunately, we have legal precedent to ask for one:

> *Then I saw in the right hand of him who was seated on the throne a scroll written within and on the back, sealed with seven seals...I saw a Lamb standing, as though it had been slain, with seven horns and with seven eyes, which are the seven spirits of God sent out into all the earth. And he went and took the scroll from the right hand of him who was seated on the throne. And when he had taken the scroll, the four living creatures and the twenty-four elders fell down before the Lamb, each holding a harp, and golden bowls full of incense, which are the prayers of the saints. And they sang a new song, saying, "Worthy are you to take the scroll and to open its seals, for you were slain, and by your blood you ransomed people for God from every tribe and language and people and nation, and you have made them a kingdom and priests to our God, and they shall reign on the earth." Then I looked, and I heard around the throne and the living creatures and the elders the voice of many angels, numbering myriads of myriads and thousands of thousands, saying with a loud voice, "Worthy is the Lamb who was slain, to receive power and wealth and wisdom and might and honor and glory and blessing!" And I heard every creature in heaven and on earth and under the earth and in the sea, and all that is in them, saying, "To him who sits on the throne and to the Lamb be blessing and honor and glory and might forever and ever!"* [12]

> *And they have conquered him by the blood of the Lamb and by the word of their testimony, for they loved not their lives even unto death.* [13]

The *word of their testimony* and the victory that is accomplished can happen within the context of a heavenly court system; it is legal testimony. A legal encounter has established the blood of the Lamb and the word of our testimony as an effective remedy to remove the enemy's rights against us, which also assures that God's judgment goes in our favor. Our conflicts with evil no longer need to be power encounters as we wrestle for healing; deliverance no longer requires screaming, flailing around and throwing up, because it is a legal encounter where the enemy is confronted with the precedent set by Jesus, the Lamb of God who takes away the sins of the world.[14]

In 2017, an angelic word delivered through Jana Green sums it up nicely:

> I am the lawmaker and the deliverer; if the works of My law would save, I would not have sent the Living Word... faith is in accordance to grace, and the promise will not be ignored. For the teachers of the law teach in error; by knowledge they assume they are better, but I have answered the ruling of the law. The most perfect court is the Court of the Cross. All things were given, but not all things received; everything for life, except when death is believed... That is why you were raised in Christ, delivered from dead works that deceive; for the law of the Spirit of life is in Christ, who has set you free from the law of sin and death. For what the law could not do, as weak as it is, was fulfilled through the flesh of His Son as an offering for the sin He condemned. All would know He is one and the law is fulfilled in this, to live by the Spirit in the truth of who He is.

But consider this: All legal testimony does not have to happen in a court. For a biblical example, all we have to do is re-visit Jesus' encounter with Satan during His forty days in the desert. With every hard-ball temptation the enemy threw at Him, Jesus countered with a scriptural truth, a testimony that could not be countered, and Satan eventually had to leave in defeat.[15] When we declare, or testify, God's own words the enemy's rights against us are as smoothly disabled as they were when he tempted Jesus:

> *How can a young man keep his way pure? By guarding it according to your word. With my whole heart I seek you; let me not wander from your commandments! I have stored up your word in my heart, that I might not sin against you. Blessed are you, O Lord; teach me your statutes! With my lips I declare all the rules of your mouth. In the way of your testimonies I delight as much*

as in all riches. I will meditate on your precepts and fix my eyes on your ways. I will delight in your statutes; I will not forget your word.[16]

This is exactly what we do each time we pray a Bible-based generational prayer. Just as surely as if we had gone into a heavenly court, the legal rights of evil are eradicated. Remember:

Submit yourselves therefore to God. Resist the devil, and he will flee from you.[17]

The sting of death is sin, and the power of sin is the law. But thanks be to God, who gives us the victory through our Lord Jesus Christ. Therefore, my beloved brothers, be steadfast, immovable, always abounding in the work of the Lord, knowing that in the Lord your labor is not in vain.[18]

Recently, I (Barbara) was sitting in my living room while praying on the phone with a lady who was thousands of miles away. I had a sense we were to do something of a legal nature and asked the Lord if we were going to court. I had to laugh because it was a new experience for me when I heard, "No, you're giving a deposition." Anywhere, anytime, the Lord has equipped us with legal remedies to use against the wiles of the enemy; our responsibility is to use them according to the direction of Holy Spirit.

---

[1] https://en.wikipedia.org/wiki/Popular_culture

[2] John 5:19 ESV

[3] See Chapter 14 of *Heaven Trek;* for more information, see http://aslansplace.3dcartstores.com/Heaven-Trek--Paul-L-Cox_p_191.html

[4] Job 11:10 ESV

[5] Psalm 50: 4-6 ESV

[6] Isaiah 2:3b-4 ESV

[7] Isaiah 33:22 ESV

[8] Hebrews 12:22-23 ESV

[9] 2 Timothy 4:8, 12 ESV

[10] Daniel 7:1, 9-10, 13-14 ESV

[11] Larry Pearson, the co-founder of Lion Sword Solutions is both a

prophet and a dear friend of Aslan's Place; his website is http//lionsword.ca

[12] Revelation 5:1, 6b-13 ESV

[13] Revelation 12:11 ESV

[14] John 1:29

[15] Matthew 4:1-11

[16] Psalm 119:9-16

[17] James 4:7

[18] 1 Corinthians 15:56-58

CHAPTER NINE

THE GODS OF THE PEOPLES

Superheroes and aliens have become ubiquitous within the world of entertainment today, to the point that rabid fans often seek to emulate them. Just attend or tune into a broadcast of Comic-Con or a Star Wars Celebration, and the sights and sounds will either cause you laugh or cry over the absurdity of it all; unless, of course, you are one of those devotees who are caught up in the hysteria, the worship, of your personal gods.

Yes, 'gods', because as fun as a particular series or movie may be to watch, or a game to play, the superheroes of today are all-to-often patterned after the mythological gods of old, the pantheon of supposedly fictional superheroes of the ancient world. Can you guess who they were? The not-so-fictional fallen sons of God, those of Old Testament fame who caused the Lord to regret having created man:

> *When man began to multiply on the face of the land and daughters were born to them, the sons of God saw that the daughters of man were attractive. And they took as their wives any they chose. Then the Lord said, "My Spirit shall not abide in man forever, for he is flesh: his days shall be 120 years." The Nephilim were on the earth in those days, and also afterward, when the sons of God came in to the daughters of man and they bore children to them. These were the mighty men who were of old, the men of renown. The Lord saw that the wickedness of man was great in the earth, and that every intention of the thoughts of his heart was only evil continually. And the Lord regretted that he had made man on the earth, and it grieved him to his heart.[1]*

The subject of the fallen sons of God was well documented by Rob Gross and Paul in *Exploring Heavenly Places, Volume 2: Revealing the sons of God,* and our purpose is not to re-visit that discussion. We will, however, go back and examine history so we can then look ahead to the battle before us.

In the mid-1990s, as Paul ministered he began discerning a spiritual pentagram on people. Historically, pentagrams were used extensively in ancient Greece and Babylonia; today we commonly see them as magic or occult symbols in satanic worship or even in mainstream religious movements and/or practices such as Mormonism, the Bahá'í Faith, and Freemasonry.[2]

During that time, Paul did a study of ancient gods of the peoples and identified three with whom the rest seem to be associated; they are Artemis, Dagon and Beelzebub/Beelzebul, also known as Baal. Together these three, known by various names from one culture to the next, seemingly form an unholy trinity that mocks the triune nature of God, Who is Father, Son and Holy Spirit. We have no desire to study these entities in such a way as to magnify their presence and power, but only wish to illuminate the truth of the spiritual horrors lurking behind the everyday evil we encounter, so we do provide a breakdown in Appendix 1 of who's who.

In 1959, Frankie Avalon's hit song, *Venus*, blasted across the airwaves and his adoring fans sang along. The lyrics detailed a young man's plea to Venus, the Roman goddess of love and beauty, to send him a girl to love, one who would also love him in return.[3] Anyone care to guess who Venus is? None other than Artemis, the great goddess of the Ephesians that caused so much trouble for Apostle Paul and his friends when the local tradesmen who crafted her idols became irate over their potential loss of income:

> *"And you see and hear that not only in Ephesus but in almost all of Asia this Paul has persuaded and turned away a great many people, saying that gods made with hands are not gods. And there is danger not only that this trade of ours may come into disrepute but also that the temple of the great goddess Artemis may be counted as nothing, and that she may even be deposed from her magnificence, she whom all Asia and the world worship." When they heard this they were enraged and were crying out, "Great is Artemis of the Ephesians!" So the city was filled with the confusion, and they rushed together*

into the theater, dragging with them Gaius and Aristarchus, Macedonians who were Paul's companions in travel. But when Paul wished to go in among the crowd, the disciples would not let him.[4]

Artemis, also known as Diana, Ashtoreth, Astarte, the Queen of Heaven and Ishtar, is the spirit behind the oh-so-popular modern-day goddess movements. She is closely aligned historically with the ancient Amazons, a predominately lesbian culture; she is worshipped by Wiccans; and is undoubtedly one of the driving forces behind abortion.[5] Not such a beautiful 'goddess of love' is she?

Next we have Dagon, popularized today in novels and films that will remain unmentioned. It was Dagon that the Philistines credited with delivering Samson into their hands; but it was in his temple that Samson made his last stand and quite literally brought down the house:

> *Then Samson called to the Lord and said, "O Lord God, please remember me and please strengthen me only this once, O God, that I may be avenged on the Philistines for my two eyes." And Samson grasped the two middle pillars on which the house rested, and he leaned his weight against them, his right hand on the one and his left hand on the other. And Samson said, "Let me die with the Philistines." Then he bowed with all his strength, and the house fell upon the lords and upon all the people who were in it. So the dead whom he killed at his death were more than those whom he had killed during his life.*[6]

The Greeks knew Dagon as Zeus; the Romans called him Jupiter; the Mesopotamians revered him as a deity depicted with the body of a fish and the head and hands of a man. He was credited with bringing life to nature through water, and wielding his perceived power over fertility and agriculture.[7] God, on the other hand, clearly showed His contempt for Dagon:

> *Then the Philistines took the ark of God and brought it into the house of Dagon and set it up beside Dagon. And when the people of Ashdod rose early the next day, behold, Dagon had fallen face*

downward on the ground before the ark of the Lord. So they took Dagon and put him back in his place. But when they rose early on the next morning, behold, Dagon had fallen face downward on the ground before the ark of the Lord, and the head of Dagon and both his hands were lying cut off on the threshold. Only the trunk of Dagon was left to him. This is why the priests of Dagon and all who enter the house of Dagon do not tread on the threshold of Dagon in Ashdod to this day.[8]

Last, but not least, we come to Beelzebub, also translated as Beelzebul. In the time of Christ, this was the common name for Satan or the devil,[9] and the Jews committed the atrocious sin of ascribing the works of Jesus to Beelzebul, thus ascribing God's supernatural deliverance and healing to the worst possible source. Jesus didn't mince any words over the matter:

Now he was casting out a demon that was mute. When the demon had gone out, the mute man spoke, and the people marveled. But some of them said, "He casts out demons by Beelzebul, the prince of demons," while others, to test him, kept seeking from him a sign from heaven. But he, knowing their thoughts, said to them, "Every kingdom divided against itself is laid waste, and a divided household falls. And if Satan also is divided against himself, how will his kingdom stand? For you say that I cast out demons by Beelzebul. And if I cast out demons by Beelzebul, by whom do your sons cast them out? Therefore they will be your judges. But if it is by the finger of God that I cast out demons, then the kingdom of God has come upon you.[10]

Again, it's nothing new; mankind is engaged in a spiritual battle that goes clear back to Eden. Israel, God's chosen people, should have known better after everything that God had done for them, and the Jews have paid a heavy price for their rebellion. The prophet, Jeremiah, recorded the Lord's intense disappointment over their idolatry:

Has a nation changed its gods, even though they are no gods? But my people have changed their glory for that which does not profit. Be appalled, O heavens, at this; be shocked, be utterly desolate, declares the Lord, for my people have committed two evils: they have forsaken me, the fountain of living waters, and hewed out cisterns for themselves, broken cisterns that can hold no water.[11]

The struggle seems to gain intensity with each day that goes by because time grows ever shorter for Beelzebub and company. Their displays may be overt and bold, such as the lighting of the Empire State Building with an image of the Hindu goddess, Kali, in April 2015. Or, they may be cleverly disguised to sound appealing using such terminology as a woman's right to choose, progressive thought, so-called errors or irrelevancy of scriptures, seductive pleasures that tickle one's fancy, dishonesty condoned in a quest for personal gain, inoffensive language or behavior, and on and on ad nauseam. And yes, it may often be difficult to discern and resist the gods' slight-of-hand maneuvers; but it definitely is possible:

For the grace of God has appeared, bringing salvation for all people, training us to renounce ungodliness and worldly passions, and to live self-controlled, upright, and godly lives in the present age, waiting for our blessed hope, the appearing of the glory of our great God and Savior Jesus Christ, who gave himself for us to redeem us from all lawlessness and to purify for himself a people for his own possession who are zealous for good works.[12]

As the children of God, as the revealed sons of God, we are responsible to hate that which is evil and cling to that which is good, for:

You are a chosen race, a royal priesthood, a holy nation, a people for his own possession, that you may proclaim the excellencies of him who called you out of darkness into his marvelous light.[13]

The enemy is indeed fierce, not to mention sneaky and cruel, but he is of the darkness; we are of the light, and Jesus, the Light of the World, overcomes the darkness every time! His own words promise:

If you abide in my word, you are truly my disciples, and you will know the truth and the truth will set you free.[14]

[1] Genesis 6:1-6 ESV

[2] https://en.wikipedia.org/wiki/Pentagram

[3] https://en.wikipedia.org/wiki/Venus_(Frankie_Avalon_song)

[4] Acts 19:26-30 ESV

[5] Price, Paula A, *The Prophet's Dictionary,* Paula Price Ministries, Tulsa, OK (2006) p65

[6] Judges 16:28-30

[7] https://en.wikipedia.org/wiki/Dagon

[8] 1 Samuel 5:2-5

[9] https://www.biblestudytools.com/dictionary/beelzebub/

[10] Luke 11:14-20

[11] Jeremiah 2:11-13

[12] Titus 2:11-14

[13] 1 Peter 2:9

[14] John 8:31b-32

CHAPTER TEN

THE ANSWER TO THE QUESTION
PART 1

Instinctively, I (Paul) answered the phone. My pulse raced. There had been an accident. "Come to Downey Community Hospital immediately." My heart was filled with trepidation. What was I to expect? What had happened? What would I say? My mind cycled through the information I had been given. A young boy on a big wheel had maneuvered between two parked cars into oncoming traffic. A Cadillac had struck him and he was in critical condition.

I arrived at the hospital to find our senior pastor standing solemnly, and I knew, even before the pastor's words confirmed my sense; the boy had died. I was instructed to drive to his home and tell an older brother that his younger brother was gone, one of the more difficult tasks of my young ministerial life.

This scenario is not unknown to pastors. Life is filled with tragedy, pain and suffering; and pastors are on the front line when life is at its worst. It is difficult enough to stand with people who are suffering, but the ensuing conversations can be unnerving. "Why did this happen?" "Why did God do this to me?" "Does God hate me this much?" "What did I do to deserve such treatment from God?" "This must be punishment from God for the terrible things I have done."

For some reason, I have not wrestled with these questions in my own life, though I do not know why. What happens in the framework of a personality that chooses not to question God? It is not as if my life, like yours, has not been filled with struggles—it certainly has.

I lived in Hawaii for three years, from ages four through six. My father was a Marine and my mom, a native New Zealander, was a stay-at-home mom. I remember one day there was great confusion; my younger brother had fallen off of a bed. Emergency personnel came and he was pronounced dead, but my young mind had no frame of reference for that information.

We then moved to the west coast of the United States, and sometime during my junior-high days my mother was diagnosed with myasthenia gravis, a neurological disease. As a high school student, I remember pushing her in a wheel chair in Oceanside, California. For years, our lives were filled with hospital visits; she would alternate between being very healthy and us receiving phone calls, "Your mother is in ICU; she cannot breathe; you need to come to the hospital right now." This happened frequently throughout my teenage years and early marriage, until she finally passed away from a heart attack in 1988.

After I married Donna, we were overjoyed with the news that she was pregnant and we were expecting our first child; but some weeks later, Donna began to bleed and finally miscarried. We were emotionally devastated.

Donna conceived again, and we were so excited when the delivery day finally came. I remember seeing our son, Brian, for the first time. What joy filled my heart! Then I looked at him more carefully, focusing on his feet; he was totally crippled with compound clubfeet. Here I was, a young father faced with the question of how I was going to take care of my infant son.

Bad news continued after Brian's birth. My mother had been taken to Long Beach Memorial Hospital, once again in crisis and in the Intensive Care Unit. Fortunately, within days she began improving and shared with her doctor about Brian's feet. Amazingly, he told her this would not be an issue because he was part of a clinic that provided free treatment for clubfeet. Almost immediately, Brian began leg brace treatments to begin correcting his legs, and a surgery during his elementary school years finally repaired the damage that had taken place in his mother's womb.

During our years at Downey First Baptist we experienced a great life, free from financial concerns. This all changed when we accepted a call to pastor the First Baptist Church of Buhl, Idaho. My salary dropped in half, and concurrently Donna started having some medical issues. The financial drought continued until we moved back to Southern California to pastor Bethany Baptist Church in Montclair, California. At times, I was under so much financial stress that I would find myself almost in a panic. These years also continued to be filled with medical issues.

I am not saying this to complain, but to point out that pastors and leaders are no different than anyone else. We live life, we have struggles, and life is not perfect for us. The question is; how does this affect our belief about God? Is He to blame for all of this pain and suffering? Again, for some reason I never blamed God and do not know why. The thought actually never occurred to me. I cannot say I had solutions to the questions people asked, but I knew internally that this was not an issue for me. Then something happened in 2018, when at the age of 74 I was startled by a new discernment. I felt what seemed to be two strong pressure points located exactly in the middle of the right and left sides on the back of my neck. I noticed the date, August 8, 2018, or 8-8-08; triple new beginning (8 commonly refers prophetically to new beginnings).

Then I remembered years back to February 8, 2008: during a ministry session at the Aslan's Place Victorian house in Hesperia, California, I was seated facing a window that framed a large pine tree in the front yard. While praying for the client, I saw a juvenile eagle rest upon the bottom branch of the pine tree. This was not a vision of spiritual eagle! Another person who was there confirmed later that she also saw it. The eagle locked eyes with me, unfurled his wings and soared off. I thought, "What is this?" It was 2-8-08, or double new beginning, but after that our lives fell apart. It was not until years later that I learned an adult eagle goes through a period of transformation or metamorphosis. At around 30 years of age, the eagle flies up to a mountain, wedges itself into the cleft of a rock and initiates a process of change. It beats out its beak, tears out its talons and plucks out its feathers, a process that takes approximately 150 days. During this period, the eagle is totally vulnerable, but when complete, the resurrected eagle can live for another forty years.

My eagle sighting and prophetic new beginning was closely followed by the 2008 recession, which hit us hard! As we went through foreclosure on our house, Donna suffered terribly with side pain that was caused by sludge in her biliary duck. I remembered this morning while writing this account that at some point in the midst of our trials someone said to me, "You are the eagle in the rock." Now I understand. It definitely was a new beginning for me in 2008, just not the kind I had expected; I was being transformed like an eagle in the rock.

Fast-forward to 8-8-18, another new beginning that I didn't understand until a few days later. Within hours of the new discernment on the back of my neck, the Holy Spirit showed me I was discerning the Lord's loving-kindness. I was not prepared for the significance of this revelation, but now realize that I have been forever changed, and understand what was not understood before. The answer to my question, "Is God to blame?" has been given.

Loving-kindness is from the Hebrew word *hesed*, translated in various Bible versions as kindness, loving-kindness, mercy, steadfast love, love, and unfailing love. It is the emotion aroused by contact with affliction. While it is the emotion that comes on others, the demonstration of love is stronger than the emotion.[1] It is God's loving-kindness.

Sometime in the early 2000s, I was in Hawaii with Donna. I woke up on a Sunday morning just after New Year's Eve and was vibrating. I went to church asking everyone, "Why am I vibrating?" I called a friend in Minnesota and she said I was vibrating at 7 hz. What did that mean? After the period of several months, the rate of vibration increased until finally it increased to 440 hz. I discovered this was the key of A above middle C, and some years later the Lord showed me it is actually 444 hz.[2] From that revelation the Lord developed a teaching based on 2 Chronicles 5:11-14:

And it came to pass when the priests came out of the Most Holy Place (for all the priests who were present had sanctified themselves, without keeping to their divisions), and the Levites who were the singers, all those of Asaph and Heman and Jeduthun, with their sons and their brethren, stood at the east end of the altar, clothed in white linen, having cymbals, stringed instruments and harps, and with them one hundred and twenty priests sounding with trumpets— indeed it came to pass, when the trumpeters and singers were as one, to make one sound to be heard in praising and thanking the LORD, and when they lifted up their voice with the trumpets and cymbals and instruments of music, and praised the LORD, saying: "For He is good, for His mercy endures forever," that the house, the house of the LORD, was filled with a cloud, so that the priests could not continue ministering because of the cloud; for the glory of the LORD filled the house of God.

For years I would speak of the sound[3] that the priest and musicians made in unity, the key words being 'sound' and 'unity'. Of course, I mentioned the phrase, "For He is good and His love endures forever," in my teaching but I was to discover that I had not yet comprehended the treasure to be found in the passage.

He is good. Months later, the reality of the word 'good' came into focus; 'good' in Hebrew is *tob* and the root refers to 'good' or 'goodness' in its broadest sense. Five general areas of meaning can be noted: 1) practical, economic, or material good, 2) abstract goodness such as desirability, pleasantness, and beauty, 3) quality or expense, 4) moral goodness, and 5) technical philosophical good.[4] Notice the emphasis on economic good!

I became aware of other passages that declared the **God is good and His love endures forever**. Notice Psalm 23:

The LORD is my shepherd; I shall not want.
He makes me to lie down in green pastures
He leads me beside the still waters.
He restores my soul;
He leads me in the paths of righteousness
For His name's sake.

Yea, though I walk through the valley of the shadow of death,
I will fear no evil;
For You are with me;
Your rod and Your staff, they comfort me.
You prepare a table before me in the presence of my enemies;
You anoint my head with oil;
My cup runs over.
Surely **goodness** *(tob) and* **mercy** *(hesed / loving-kindness) shall follow me*
All the days of my life;
And I will dwell in the house of the LORD *Forever.*

As a Baptist pastor I'd preached through the book of Lamentations, which illustrates that when we feel pain God is not unmoved by our struggles. Each of the verses of the first chapter begins with the chronological letters in the Hebrew alphabet, and the second chapter repeats this same pattern. Chapter 3, however, repeats each letter three times. It is as if there is a crescendo in the intensity of pain and suffering, and then in the exact middle of the book is a sudden declaration in 3:22-25:

Through the Lord's **mercies** *(hesed) we are not consumed,*
Because His compassions fail not.
They are new every morning;
Great is Your faithfulness.
"The Lord is my portion," says my soul,
"Therefore, I hope in Him!"
The Lord is **good** *(tob) to those who wait for Him,*
To the soul who seeks Him.

You may now understand what I discovered. When we confront the reality of pain and suffering, God is not the problem. Scripture is clear, **"He is good and His loving-kindness endures forever."** This is the very nature of Elohim; this is His character; this is His central attribute. He is not the author of sin, pain and suffering. We have believed an evil report; we have been totally deceived; we have accepted the 'mob view' of God, believing, "It is His fault! God is NOT good." Say it often enough and loud enough, and everyone will believe this lie. But what is the truth?

The truth is, **He is good and His loving-kindness endures forever.** So, we have a problem. How do we reconcile our reality to this truth?

---

[1] [1] Harris, R. L. (1999). 698 חסד. R. L. Harris, G. L. Archer Jr., & B. K. Waltke (Eds.), *Theological Wordbook of the Old Testament* (electronic ed., p. 305). Chicago: Moody Press.

[2] Ezekiel 44:4

[3] Notice that the singers and musicians did not sing a song but made a sound.

[4] Bowling, A. (1999). 793 טוֹב. R. L. Harris, G. L. Archer Jr., & B. K. Waltke (Eds.), *Theological Wordbook of the Old Testament* (electronic ed., p. 345). Chicago: Moody Press.

CHAPTER ELEVEN

THE ANSWER TO THE QUESTION

PART 2

Growing up in the Southern Baptist Church, and later as an adult in American Baptist Churches, I was taught different versions of supposed truth; the reason for pain and suffering is, "God has His reasons." "God did this to you so that you would become more mature." "God is causing this to happen so He can work out all things for His glory." "God gave this to you." "God allowed this to happen for some unknown reason." But how can this be if **He is good and His loving-kindness endures forever?**

When a disaster happens, we hear theologians, biblical scholars, and friends say, "Well God had His reasons for doing that." Or, when a personal tragedy happens, when children or spouses die, when all manner of terrible physical things occur, time and again we hear people say, "Well God had His reasons." That has to be a lie because, **He is good and His love endures forever**. So contrary to what we've been conditioned to believe, whenever anything bad happens our first thought and words must be, **"He is good and His loving-kindness endures forever."** This is the truth! No matter what happens, our first response should always be the same.

Not convinced? Look at some scriptural proof:

> Deuteronomy 7:9—*Therefore know that the LORD your God, He is God, the faithful God who keeps covenant and* **mercy** *(hesed) for a thousand generations with those who love Him and keep His commandments.*

> Psalm 85:10—**Mercy** *(hesed) and truth have met together; Righteousness and peace have kissed.*

80

Psalm 86:15—*But You, O Lord, are a God full of compassion, and gracious, Longsuffering and abundant in* **mercy** *(hesed) and truth.*

It would seem we now have a theological problem. Why do bad things happen? Why am I suffering? Why am I not totally better? Why do I have financial difficulty? Why is this going on? Theology has long taught about the permissive will of God, explaining that He allows certain circumstances to occur for His reasons that are totally unknown to us. Only when we are in Heaven will we understand. I believed and taught this for many years, but not anymore; for **He is good and His loving-kindness endures forever**. How do we reconcile all of this?

In 2018, Jana Green joined me in a prayer session for a long-term client who has suffered greatly, especially during her early years. Often, we would hear her ask, "Why did God allow this to happen?" Our response was usually silence, for what answer to that question can ever bring a solution? I now have an answer, for during one session Jana received a word from the Lord in response to her question, "I did not do this nor did I allow it to happen."

I was stunned! What? This can't possibly be true! I have such respect for Jana but thought, "I am not sure she is right about this." Over the course of several weeks, Jana would be delivering amazing words from the Lord and in the midst of them these same words came, "I did not do this nor did I allow this evil to happen to you." How can this be?

I felt that what Jana said was tied to the nature of law, so I consulted a few attorney friends and talked to a professor of law from a local university. "Tell me about the nature of law and this phrase from the Lord." They could not help with my question. "Tell me about the nature of law in regard to this phrase, 'I did not do this nor did I allow this evil to happen to you.'" No response.

Later in 2018, I was in Collingwood, Canada, sharing what the Lord had said through Jana when suddenly the Holy Spirit started speaking and I finally understood: You do not blame the law maker when you disobey a law. The law is the law. It is set. There are consequences to breaking the law. When someone breaks the law, others are impacted by that decision. We do not blame the lawmakers. If I get pulled over by the police I do not say, "Why did the State of California do this to me?" I've not said that once. Why? Because the law is neutral.

Let's look at one of God's laws, the Law of Gravity. If you decide to deny the Law of Gravity, and in defiance to that law shout at God in rebellion and step off of a roof, the law will operate the way it is supposed to act. We can complain about the law, but the reality is that it functions to keep us safe. Otherwise, we would fly off into the sky with no ability to come back down. Now, we could say as we are rapidly descending to the ground, "Why, God, are You doing this to me?" But that question is irrelevant; the more correct question is, "Why are you so dumb to do that?"

We have a whole book, the Bible, which is our guidebook about things that we can do to stay out of trouble, but I can hear the questions already, "Yes, but what about this? What about that?" Of course, this is complicated because God has created a complex world, but truth is truth. The first and central truth is that **God is good and His loving-kindness endures forever**. We start here. Period.

When did the lie start, the lie that God was to blame? It started at the beginning; it started when the enemy questioned God's goodness, "Did God really say?" This is implied by the statement, "God is not really good because He is keeping from you the things that you really need to have, and want to have." From the very beginning, the enemy has shouted loudly, "He is not good and He is not loving!" For centuries, we have bought into the lie, wrestling with questions about sin and evil and pain and suffering. But the final answer to the "Why?" questions is not a philosophical or religious response; it is a statement of truth, **"He is good and His loving-kindness endures forever."** This is who my God is.

When will we finally blame the enemy? When do we take responsibility for our sin, and for the consequences of our sin and generational sin? When do we finally declare what is Truth, and stop repeating the lie that God is not good? Truth is waiting to be revealed, and Jana Green received this word in 2019:

> Truth always works with love, and you grow up in all aspects of Him. Truth is shattering the paradigm that caused unbelief. What is the paradigm that causes unbelief? "He is not good." A sound that resonates holds a false shield in place; it blocks the understanding of the grace of God, but I am shattering the opinion of the world view and their governmental laws; I, Truth, reveal the knowledge of His will in all wisdom and understanding. You will breakthrough to what is His; you will shut out the noise that blocks the sound of love spoken in Truth, for from the beginning of salvation the Spirit of Faith is in the Truth. You have a sound that needs to be heard so even the disobedient will be delivered and My mercy, My loving-kindness, will be fulfilled. I will show the way of Truth, which falls in My love, in My abundant loving-kindness where faith is trust.

Look again at 2 Chronicles 5:11-14. I've mentioned repeatedly that the key is, **"He is good and His loving-kindness endures forever."** But notice that this was declared in the atmosphere of total unity; the musicians, the priest and all present were in complete agreement, of one accord. What truth were they unified around? They were not in agreement about some set of theological or religious tenets; they were unified around **one** truth, **"For He is good and His loving-kindness endures forever."**

Is this what it means to be unified with all believers, to be one mind and one spirit? Is this what it means to be unified within ourselves? In 2017, the Lord showed us that we must first be in unity within ourselves so that our spirit and soul parts that have been scattered in the length, width, height, depth, and in the stars are returned to us so that we are one in Christ. It occurred to me that we cannot declare, **"He is good and His loving-kindness endures forever,"** when we are not in unity within ourselves because those wounded parts that are in so much pain are not willing to declare God's goodness.

Jana Green received another word:

> All things manifest from who I AM. This rule of peace and loving-kindness is My strong right hand, for I am rich in loving-kindness because of My great love. Even the sound of My voice is anchored in mercy. Like the Ark of the Covenant with the pure gold, it is what enables the scribes to re-write the hearts and connect love. Hope will never disappoint from a heart in My love.

Then I started having a cascading revelation. Remember that Psalm 23 ends with, "Surely goodness and loving-kindness will follow you all the days of your life." It's right there, and I believe the Lord wants to release this revelation like a flood upon the earth, **"He is good and His loving-kindness endure forever."**

Then signs and wonders came! Donna and I were in Cranbrook, Canada. Nestled there in the middle of the Rocky Mountains, is a spectacular piece of property cradling a glorious house. Our host had put us in the third-floor master suite, a garage-sized room with an adjoining master bath larger than our living room at home. In the center of the bathroom is a large Jacuzzi bathtub, and on either side of the bathroom are two large make-up centers with tables and chairs.

I woke up in the middle of the night to find that the bathtub had turned on and the jets were spraying hot water into the tub. With difficulty, I was finally able to turn off the water and went back to sleep. The following day all was well, but that night the bathtub again turned itself on. After repeated attempts, I was able to turn off the water and return to bed. Later, I woke to use the facilities and stepping out of the bed landed in a pool of water. I panicked! Water had flowed out of this large bathroom into the center of this large bedroom, and I realized that soon the water would be running down the double-sided staircase. I pictured a magnificent waterfall cascading into the floor below so I ran to the bathtub and tried to turn it off, but repeated attempts failed. Finally, I called our host and told him of the problem. He came to the room and disassembled the water valve so the water stopped. Later that morning the plumber came to diagnose the problem, but all possible solutions did not match what had happened. The plumber finally left the house; but when he returned to his truck, his radio automatically turned on, even though the keys were still in his hands. He came back to the front door and told our host, "I don't know what is going on here but there is super-weird spiritual stuff happening in that house!" Our host later said that this had never happened before, nor has it happened since.

Three months later at the end of September 2018, I was in Gulf Shores, Alabama, staying in a condo on the seashore overlooking the Gulf of Mexico. Tropical storm Gordon was about to hit directly, with a forecast that it would become a hurricane by landfall. That was not the only problem though; I had walked into the second of two bedrooms and stepped into water next to the bathroom. Looking down, I could see no obvious reason for it but the water appeared to be coming up out of the tile floor. The weather was very humid so I surmised that condensation was seeping through and placed a towel down to soak it up. But later, water started coming up from the floor in the master bedroom too, and even more water came up in the second bedroom. I called our host and reported the problem. Three days later, a repairman came and reported that there are no pipes in any of the floors of the condo. Nevertheless, the water continued to bubble up from the floor until I left. My host reported that this has not happened in the twenty years she has owned the condo, nor has it happened since we left. I might also add that tropical storm Gordon hit land with 70 mph winds, never reaching hurricane force, and that year was the 70th anniversary of Israel.

In Kaneohe, HI, in November 2018, I was preparing to go to Mountain View Community Church to preach. I went into the bathroom and noticed water was coming up from the floor around the toilet, and dirty water was pouring into the bathtub. I thought, "Here we go again," and called the owner of the property to report the problem. It turned out that the dirty water in the bathtub had come from the unit behind ours, but why the clean water on the floor?

A sign and wonder—a sign that caused me to wonder! Then the Lord reminded me of Habakkuk 2:14:

> *For the earth will be filled with the knowledge of the glory of the LORD as the waters cover the sea.*

What is this knowledge? **He is good and His love endures forever.**

Return once more to 2 Chronicles 5:11-13:

> *And it came to pass when the priests came out of the Most Holy Place (for all the priests who were present had sanctified themselves,* **without keeping to their divisions)**, *and the Levites who were the singers, all those of Asaph and Heman and Jeduthun, with their sons and their brethren, stood at the east end of the altar, clothed in white linen, having cymbals, stringed instruments and harps, and with them one hundred and twenty priests sounding with trumpets—indeed it came to pass, when the trumpeters and singers* **were as one**, *to make* **one sound** *to be heard in praising and thanking the LORD, and when they lifted up their voice with the trumpets and cymbals and instruments of music, and praised the LORD, saying:* **"For He is good, For His mercy endures forever."**

Then God's glory fell!

CHAPTER TWELVE

THE GLORIOUS ONES:
PART 1

The unfolding revelation of the glorious ones fits well into the Lord's recurring pattern of introducing us to small bits and pieces of knowledge and understanding over extended periods of time. A play-by-play account between Paul and Rob Gross provides a humorous introduction to the topic, as taught on November 11, 2018, at Mountain View Community Church in Kaneohe, Hawaii. Rob had just introduced Paul:

> (Paul) Rob, you're going to have to come back up here; Rob is trying to leave, but he's not going to make it. This week, I've been re-visiting something that I did not know a whole lot about when it was first discerned, and there's a funny story about what happened between Rob and me so I'll have him tell the story. When he first told it a couple of years ago at a school, I said to him (this is the truth!), "I did not do that." He said, "Paul, you did do that." I said, "I do not remember that, and I did not do that," and he said, "Yes you did!"

> (Rob) I don't remember what year it was. Do you?

> (Paul) It was a long time ago.

> (Rob) Yes, so a long time ago we had just shipped you back to California on American Airlines, and that night

you called to say that you had gotten home. Actually, you had fallen asleep but had gotten up because you wanted me to know—this is so bizarre! He said real briefly, "Rob…"

(Paul interrupted) I was asleep, and I really deny that I did this!

(Rob) He said, "Rob the glorious ones are in the lava tubes. Ok, that's all I have; goodnight." Then he hung up, so the next time we spoke I said, "Oh, so what about this?"

(Paul) No, it was a couple years later when you told me at a school.

(Rob) Well, you said it!

With the comedic interchange over, Paul's teaching began in Jude 1:5-10, and he commented that the scriptures that would be addressed are probably some of the most complex passages in the Word of God:

Now I want to remind you, although you once fully knew it, that Jesus, who saved a people out of the land of Egypt, afterward destroyed those who did not believe. And the angels who did not stay within their own position of authority, but left their proper dwelling, he has kept in eternal chains under gloomy darkness until the judgment of the great day—just as Sodom and Gomorrah and the surrounding cities, which likewise indulged in sexual immorality and pursued unnatural desire, serve as an example by undergoing a punishment of eternal fire. Yet in like manner these people also, relying on their dreams, defile the flesh, reject authority, and blaspheme the glorious ones. But when the archangel Michael, contending with the devil, was disputing about the body of Moses, he did not presume to pronounce a blasphemous judgment, but said, "The Lord rebuke you." But these people blaspheme all that they do not understand, and they are destroyed by all that they, like unreasoning animals, understand instinctively.

2 Peter 2 provides a whole list of some really bad, sinful behaviors, and then you come to verse 10:

> *...and especially those who indulge in the lust of defiling passion and despise authority. Bold and willful, they do not tremble as they blaspheme the <u>glorious ones</u>...*

The Greek word for 'glorious ones' is *doxa,* which denotes 'opinion', and is always good in the New Testament; therefore it means praise, honor and glory.[1] The issue of speaking evil is to blaspheme, so in the passage above they blaspheme the glorious ones.

Some time ago, I felt like the Lord said that the glorious ones are living light beings. Initially I thought they were living light, but at a recent academy at Aslan's Place I suddenly realized that this is not quite correct; actually, they are vibrations and each vibration is a living being. String theory says that behind all matter is vibration or, put another way, all elementary particles are manifestations of the vibrations of one-dimensional strings.[2] I would suggest each one of those strings is a glorious one, or a *doxa*; they are very small beings.

In Genesis 1:2, we see that during God's creation of the heavens and the earth, He said, "Let there be light." Light is the visible representation of vibration; furthermore, sound is the audible representation of vibration and frequency is a measure of the vibration; so the reality seems to be that we are going back to vibrations in the beginning when God essentially said, "Let there be vibrations." If this is true, and it is, what does it mean to blaspheme the vibrations?

In the Old Testament, the word blaspheme is the word *naats,*[3] which means to despise, to abhor, blaspheme, treat with disdain or contempt, to rebel against authority, to hate, not believing in the Lord, to say sharp things, reproach, scorn, belittle, deprecate. Please understand this; to deprecate God's power and authority to carry out His threats, or to say that God is not going to do what He says He's going to do, is to blaspheme. It is a contentious view of

God that refers to abusive, evil speech, and is the strongest form of personal mockery; such blasphemy that mistakes His true nature and violates or doubts his power is against the name of God. Now it gets really complex.

Matthew 12:31-32 is a very interesting passage, and if you are in church for about 10 minutes you'll get to the point in a discussion about what it means to blaspheme the Holy Spirit because this is a sin that is unforgivable:

> *Therefore I tell you, every sin and blasphemy will be forgiven people, but the blasphemy against the Spirit will not be forgiven. And whoever speaks a word against the Son of Man will be forgiven, but whoever speaks against the Holy Spirit will not be forgiven, either in this age or in the age to come.*

Remember, to blaspheme is to belittle, speak evil of or deny the power of God; but look at the context in the preceding verses, Matthew 12: 22-28:

> *Then a demon-oppressed man who was blind and mute was brought to him, and he healed him, so that the man spoke and saw. And all the people were amazed, and said, "Can this be the Son of David?" But when the Pharisees heard it, they said, "It is only by Beelzebul, the prince of demons, that this man casts out demons." Knowing their thoughts, he said to them, "Every kingdom divided against itself is laid waste, and no city or house divided against itself will stand. And if Satan casts out Satan, he is divided against himself. How then will his kingdom stand? And if I cast out demons by Beelzebul, by whom do your sons cast them out? Therefore they will be your judges. But if it is by the Spirit of God that I cast out demons, then the kingdom of God has come upon you.*

Jesus delivered and healed someone, and the non-believers were excited—they got it! But the Pharisees claimed it had only been done by Beelzebul, or Beelzebub, the lord of the demons; and the demons are little gods, or fallen sons of God. 'Beelzebub' is the Greek translation for the Hebrew 'Baal', and Baal is the same entity as Moloch; so regardless of the name used, the reference is to the fallen sons of God. The Pharisees were basically saying, "Look at this Jesus; he does this by the power of the fallen sons of God, by Beelzebub, by Satan." But Jesus' response makes it clear that when one attributes the power and works of the Holy Spirit in deliverance and healing to the devil, that is blasphemy against the Spirit. So to be clear, our discussion here is about blasphemy of the glorious ones (translated as dignitaries in the NKJV); it's blasphemy against the *doxa,* not the Holy Spirit.

While I was pondering all of this, the Lord started downloading information while I was just sitting and watching TV, minding my own business. All of a sudden, I felt the glorious ones and and I was going, "Oh, oh, oh, oh, oh, oh, ooohhh, uh-oh, uh-oh." To begin sorting it all out, look at the order of creation; first we have Father, Son and Holy Spirit, who are from everlasting to everlasting.[4] To think about that makes my head hurt! How can it be that He always is, no-one has created Him, and He is everlasting? Then this everlasting God spoke and created when He said, "Let there be light." In other words, let there be vibrations, let there be the glorious ones. Then He created the sun, moon and stars. Light came before the celestial bodies, so we're not talking about those sources of light but about vibrations. Only after the creation of vibrations did He create the earth, planets, animals, and mankind. Is that not correct?

So then man came along, and Adam and Eve were placed in this Garden that God had created. Eventually, they ended up standing by the Tree of the Knowledge of Good and Evil and the serpent was also there:

> But the serpent said to the woman, "You will not surely die. For God knows that when you eat of it your eyes will be opened, and you will be like God, knowing good and evil." So when the woman saw that the tree was good for food, and that it was a delight to the eyes, and that the tree was to be desired to make one wise, she took of its fruit and ate, and she also gave some to her husband who was with her, and he ate.[5]

91

Actually, I think the serpent's words should be translated, "You'll be like the gods," referring to the fallen sons of God who already knew about good and evil. Also, Eve didn't eat the fruit and then go off somewhere to find Adam and tell him about it. No, he was there, listening to the conversation as a willing participant. Women should not believe the enduring lie that it's all their fault.

James 1:17 tells us that God is the Father of lights, or vibrations; so what happened was a sequence in which our everlasting God created light/vibrations and then proceeded to create the heavens, the earth and all that dwells upon it, including mankind who succumbed to sin. Then, in 2 Peter and Jude, the sin issue was compounded by blasphemy against the glorious ones. We must understand that man twists things around and declares not that God created light/vibrations, but that the light/vibrations are God. Morphing into familiar concepts of today, man professes that God is no longer personal but is simply a universal life force or, in Star Wars terminology, the Force. Transcendental Meditation teaches that we can tap into this force in order to become wise, and when we succumb to that fallacy we dislodge the glorious ones from Creator God; we say that we will now worship them as our gods.

When I started looking into this, I got the word 'Gnosticism', which was not defined as a hierarchy until well after Jude and 2 Peter were written, but my research indicated that the roots of Gnosticism existed within in the early church, and we have all been duped by it down through the years. Going forward, we'll look into this   history   in   greater   detail.

---

[1] https://biblehub.com/greek/1391.htm

[2] https://www.merriam-webster.com/dictionary/string%20theory

[3] https://biblehub.com/hebrew/5006.htm

[4] Psalm 90:2

[5] Genesis 3:4-6

CHAPTER THIRTEEN
THE GLORIOUS ONES:
PART 2

The last chapter ended with the shocking statement that throughout church history many Christians have been duped into believing a lie. Our examination of how this has happened will take us back to before the time of Christ.

Buddha probably lived somewhere around 600-500 BC; he was born in upper India (now Nepal) and was thought to have been conceived during a dream when a white elephant with six white tusks entered his mother's side.[1] During that same time period, the Children of Israel were living in captivity in Babylon; Daniel was there and he began receiving information about what would happen during the end times, including the revelation of the 70 weeks. I believe that the enemy recognized the outline of God's plans to the end of the age at that point and figured, "I need to develop other religions that will counteract whoever this One is who is going to be cut off; and I need to make sure during the 70th week, the final week, that I am successful and God is not." So, along came Buddha, and with him began all this esoteric mumbo jumbo we encounter today—buying into a universal life force (i.e., Chi, Ki or Qi energy, etc.), which has spread into Star Wars, other entertainment, and is pervasive throughout all types of media. Under the guise of New Age thinking, it subtly creeps even into Christianity.

It's interesting that before I got into all this strange discernment and deliverance stuff, I became intrigued by the New Age ideologies and started studying its beliefs and practices. It's all about tapping into this universal life force; it's the wisdom of Yoda's profound sayings; it's human wisdom; it's blaspheming the vibrations, professing that the vibrations are god and that He is not God; it's saying that the impersonal force is now our god.

Equally disturbing is yoga, which has become very popular. But what is yoga? We think we know, but let me go back to the roots of Gnosticism because it all comes together.[2] Gnosticism says that all matter is evil and there is an unknowable god who gave rise to many lesser spirit beings called Aeons, which are the glorious ones. This belief claims that the creator of the material universe is not even the supreme god, but is an inferior spirit; in other words, the creation came out of something that was itself created. Furthermore, it does not deal with sin, for all that is thought necessary to achieve salvation is for one to get in touch with the secret knowledge that is based on personal experience or perception, or *gnosis*. Gnosticism's remote, supreme godhead is the highest divinity, followed the lower divine beings, and to have this inward knowing is considered wisdom. Obviously, adherents to this belief have not understood the truth of Romans 16:25-27:

> *Now to him who is able to strengthen you according to my gospel and the preaching of Jesus Christ, according to the revelation of the mystery that was kept secret for long ages but has now been disclosed and through the prophetic writings has been made known to all nations, according to the command of the eternal God, to bring about the obedience of faith—to the only wise God be glory forevermore through Jesus Christ! Amen.*

Yoga is closely aligned with Gnosticism. The word 'yoga' actually means 'to join with', referring to the Hindu gods. Friends, you cannot have Christian yoga. There is simply no such thing, for a Christian is called to have no other gods before Him; to join with them, even though a series of stretching exercises that the world has convinced us are perfectly ok, is blasphemy of the glorious ones because it attributes the works of the one-and-only Creator God to the created glorious ones.

Romans 1:18-32 clarifies the issue in no uncertain terms:

> *For the wrath of God is revealed from heaven against all ungodliness and unrighteousness of men, who by their unrighteousness suppress the truth. For what can be known about God is plain to them, because God has shown it to them. For his invisible attributes,*

namely, his eternal power and divine nature, have been clearly perceived, ever since the creation of the world, in the things that have been made. So they are without excuse. For although they knew God, they did not honor him as God or give thanks to him, but they became futile in their thinking, and their foolish hearts were darkened. <u>Claiming to be wise, they became fools</u>, and exchanged the glory of the immortal God for images resembling mortal man and birds and animals and creeping things. Therefore God gave them up in the lusts of their hearts to impurity, to the dishonoring of their bodies among themselves, because they exchanged the truth about God for a lie and worshiped and served the creature rather than the Creator, who is blessed forever! Amen.

For this reason God gave them up to dishonorable passions. For their women exchanged natural relations for those that are contrary to nature; and the men likewise gave up natural relations with women and were consumed with passion for one another, men committing shameless acts with men and receiving in themselves the due penalty for their error. And since they did not see fit to acknowledge God, God gave them up to a debased mind to do what ought not to be done. They were filled with all manner of unrighteousness, evil, covetousness, malice. They are full of envy, murder, strife, deceit, maliciousness. They are gossips, slanderers, haters of God, insolent, haughty, boastful, inventors of evil, disobedient to parents, foolish, faithless, heartless, ruthless. Though they know God's righteous decree that those who practice such things deserve to die, they not only do them but give approval to those who practice them.

After much study, I realized what has happened; because the Holy Spirit is a person and not simply a force, when you dislodge or disconnect the glorious ones from the true and personal Godhead, then everything starts floating aimlessly around and chaos ensues. People begin justifying all their sins by saying, "These sins are ok because it doesn't matter what we do in the flesh." You see, people think sin doesn't matter because there's no longer any anchor for truth; it has is now been attached to the creation rather than the Creator

I also looked into freemasonry, which is all about the light. A candidate is 'brought to the light', and 'let there be light' is the motto of the craft. When one goes through an initiation, the supposed truth of masonry is said to have found entrance to the divine, and the person is declared to be enlightened. Indeed, the masonic is all about enlightenment, but Ephesians 1:17-21 contradicts that mentality:

> ...that the God of our Lord Jesus Christ, the Father of glory, may give you the Spirit of wisdom and of revelation in the knowledge of him, having the eyes of your hearts enlightened, that you may know what is the hope to which he has called you, what are the riches of his glorious inheritance in the saints, and what is the immeasurable greatness of his power toward us who believe, according to the working of his great might that he worked in Christ when he raised him from the dead and seated him at his right hand in the heavenly places, far above all rule and authority and power and dominion, and above every name that is named, not only in this age but also in the one to come.

We are to be enlightened through Christ, who is a person; and our enlightenment develops out of a personal relationship with Father, Son and Holy Spirit. Meanwhile, freemasons call themselves sons of light because they believe that they are entitled to possess the true meaning of knowledge; to them it's all about knowledge and wisdom and being smart. They are said to be wise, but are they really? No. In spite of all their talk of wisdom, they are only wise in their own eyes, for *claiming to be wise they became fools.*

Adherents to the philosophy of a universal life force believe we are all filled with this force, or energy, which is the essence of our being, our conscience, our soul. As the flow of this energy moves through our physical, emotional and spiritual bodies it can become unbalanced, stagnant and blocked. When this happens we experience what is called dis-ease that, as the hyphenated spelling suggests, refers to a lack of ease or harmony; it is the inability of one's life force energy to flow freely.

These subversive, false beliefs permeate our society. When one practices yoga, a spiritual agreement is entered into that says he/she wants to tap into the universal life force. I have friends who are chiropractors or massage therapists but do not believe in their profession's common teaching that the body needs to be aligned to the universal life force or Chi; they learn about aligning with the chakra points so the energy can flow, which comes right back to Buddhism.[3]

Reiki is another subtle method that often creeps in unawares. Reiki is the Japanese name for the universal life force, also known as Ki or Chi, the supposed subtle energy that enlivens all beings. One ex-reiki master says, "Reiki is something that is very mis-stated, and misunderstood, by those outside of the Reiki circle. Having been in it, I can tell you everything you need to know. I will tell you right up front that it was a hard one to shake, that it was VERY real and beneficial, but that it is decidedly non-Christian. I highly recommend anyone looking into it to just stop. Prayer is very powerful, and is our direct link to God through Christ. If we petition directly for healing, it may come. If we have faith that it WILL come, our chances are far better. As with anything we are to test, does Reiki point either the practitioner or the client to Christ? No. Big no. It uses a Universal energy that is non-personal and can be manipulated. You can pray to God, to the Earth Mother, to Mother/Father God, etc. But it in fact leads you AWAY from Christ." [4]

All of these corrupted belief systems may have existed in our ancestors, in which case they have come down through our generational lines. Then we find, often to our surprise, that we have accepted, believed and practiced family traditions that are false. Or, we may have developed our own false beliefs based on what we see, hear or experience in daily life. For example, it's not uncommon as we minister to people to hear them say such things as, "Yoga is being practiced in my church, but we do Christian yoga." Or, "There are lots of masons who are members of my church or family, and they are really good people so it must be ok." Wrong! Such false assumptions/statements are nothing short of blasphemy.

Our friends are watching *Poldark* on Masterpiece Theater, and the predominant theme that runs through the show is adultery. The hero, Poldark, commits adultery; the young heroine, Demelza, commits adultery; everyone is committing adultery. Sitting there during a broadcast, I thought, "Oh my goodness, when we tap into these lies about the universal life force we are committing adultery against our Bridegroom, against Jesus. Let me say this again; when we buy into a universal life force lie, when we buy into man's wisdom, we are committing adultery against our Bridegroom Jesus.

I want to say this very carefully—when we are intimate with our spouse, coming together with love during the marriage act and looking eye-to-eye at one another, if we allow some other thought to come in and turn our focus away from her or his eyes to gaze elsewhere, that is adultery. In similar fashion, how dare we commit adultery against our Bridegroom and then try to justify it! We justify sin; we justify wrong doing; we justify our belief systems; we justify compromise; all because we have disconnected ourselves from the Word of God and are defiantly explaining away His Truth. Meanwhile, we blaspheme the glorious ones by saying and believing that they are the ones who are going to give us wisdom, not the Father, Son and Holy Spirit."

We can have generational contamination, we can have personal contamination, and unfortunately we're also being contaminated by our educational system and by the belief systems of the people in Hollywood—the entertainment industry. I enjoy watching programs and I'm not against television or movies, but we need to start to get a clue about what's really going on, what's really being taught, what's being handed over to us as truth. We need to recognize the deception that lurks in even the most seemingly family-friendly shows, not to mention the blatant disregard for God's righteous and just principles in everything from cartoons to news to talk shows to X-rated movies. We get so impressed because people seem wise, yet their wisdom is not tied to the Word of God; so it should be no surprise to see that everything is now adrift in what we call situational ethics. We have become a country totally divided in half, and it's not an issue of Democrats versus Republicans, left versus right, or liberal versus conservative; it's an issue of truth. Our debate is not over which party line or school of thought is correct; our debate is in regard to the validity of the Word of God.

What is truth? Many people seem to struggle over that question, but it's really very simple; truth is the Father, the Son and the Holy Spirit, and they are persons Who want to have a personal relationship with us. They are not some sort of impersonal and unknowable force that's going to give us a kind of esoteric, inner knowledge or wisdom so we can all achieve enlightenment and become ascended masters. Truth is not about becoming another Yoda; it's about becoming a redeemed and revealed son or daughter of God who enjoys a personal, loving relationship with our Savior, our Bridegroom, Jesus. Truth is about placing our focus only on Him and no longer on anything else; truth is saying, "No matter what happens, I will focus on You, Jesus, for You are good and Your love endures forever. I will only speak truth, for I don't care what anybody else teaches or speaks or believes. Truth is truth, His Word is truth, and truth cannot exist aside from the person of the Holy Spirit.

In *Poldark*, Ross Poldark and Demelza are talking, and they know that each of them has committed adultery. Their discussion revolves around whether or not it is possible to give just a part of one's heart to someone else. One says yes, but they know it is not true. Both are full of excuses about why they have behaved as they have, and there is an acknowledgement of how wounding the act of adultery is. Finally, the understanding comes that when you become one with someone in a marriage, they must have your whole heart and you must have theirs. You are not content to say, "Ok, I will give you 75% of me, but the other 25% is for another person." This is what Jesus is asking of us; He wants 100% of our devotion. Why? Is He asking this because He is a mean God and doesn't want us to have any fun? No, He's a loving God who doesn't want us to ruin our lives because our hearts are divided against the Lord. When hearts are divided within a marriage, the marriage becomes dysfunctional and may even be destroyed. When hearts are divided in a relationship with God, everything in life starts to fall apart and as it crumbles, sin becomes more and more prevalent, which in turn causes more and more wreckage. He knows that when He is the focus of your praise, the focus of your adoration, the focus of your love, the focus of everything, then life's details suddenly line up and there is order. When He is your all-in-all and you are one-and-One, then you are healthy, wealthy, and can have God's wisdom rather than your own.

---

[1] https://en.wikipedia.org/wiki/Gautama_Buddha

[2] https://en.wikipedia.org/wiki/Gnosticism

[3] We believe that the Chakras and a corruption of the Godly concept known as the Seven Eyes of the Lord. More information and a link to the *Prayer to Rescind the Evils Associated With Buddhism* can be accessed at https://aslansplace.com/language/en/discerning-the-seven-eyes-of-the-lord/

[4] https://aslansplace.com/language/en/reiki-and-biblical-discernment/

CHAPTER FOURTEEN

THE STATE OF THE CHURCH

The President of the United States of America delivers a State of the Union address each year to a joint session of the United States Congress. The speech typically addresses current socio-economic issues in the country; it also allows the president to propose a legislative agenda and highlight national priorities. People all over the nation and around the world can tune in to listen or watch, either in real time or after-the-fact in pre-recorded broadcasts. Given the sorry state of deception that has infiltrated the Church, wouldn't be nice if someone would put out a State of the Church address? But oh, wait—hmmm—someone already has! It was dictated to the Apostle John, who wrote it down for delivery to the Church of his day, specifically to seven churches in Asia.

As the State of the Union address is often controversial, so is the book of Revelation. Biblical scholars have often debated whether it's meant to be preterist, futurist, historicist or idealist.[1] Personally, I (Barbara) prefer the simple truth of Revelation 1:1-3 as my interpretative guide:

> *The revelation of Jesus Christ, which God gave him to show to his servants the things that must soon take place. He made it known by sending his angel to his servant John, who bore witness to the word of God and to the testimony of Jesus Christ, even to all that he saw. Blessed is the one who reads aloud the words of this prophecy, and blessed are those who hear, and who keep what is written in it, for the time is near.*

So far, we have detailed a number of issues that we see confronting the Church in this present battle. So now, let's look a bit more closely at what Jesus has to say about the state of His Church today, because those letters to the seven churches are as relevant now as when they were first received and written down by John the Apostle.

Why did the Lord specify that the letters be written specifically to Ephesus, Smyrna, Pergamum, Thyatira, Sardis, Philadelphia and Laodicea? Certainly there were other churches at the time that needed either a loving rebuke or gentle encouragement. How about Corinth? Apostle Paul definitely had to address some doctrinal issues there! Or what of the Galatians to whom he wrote:

> *I am astonished that you are so quickly deserting him who called you in the grace of Christ and are turning to a different gospel—not that there is another one, but there are some who trouble you and want to distort the gospel of Christ.²*

Peter addressed Christians who had been scattered far and wide as a result of persecution:

> *To those who are elect exiles of the Dispersion in Pontus, Galatia, Cappadocia, Asia, and Bithynia...³*

There can be no doubt that a lot more than seven individual congregations needed to hear the Lord's message, both then and now. Biblically, the number seven represents completeness, wholeness or perfection, so I suspect that Jesus hand-picked the first seven recipients of His Revelation because those particular churches embodied the full message that He wanted to deliver to His whole Church.

A couple of nights ago, I finished editing and inserting the chapters about the glorious ones into this manuscript with no thought of adding anything else—the rest of the book had already been completed and was ready to go and I was ready to move on to the next project. The following morning, during my morning quiet time, I was off on what I thought was a totally different track but the Spirit led me on a biblical journey that wasn't part of my regular reading plan. I ended up in Revelation 2 and 3, and was astonished at how it confirmed everything Paul spoke of in the last two chapters, not to mention much of the rest of this book. Thus, here we are.

Jesus had nothing but praise and encouragement for only two of the churches, Smyrna and Philadelphia. Both had endured much, but had persevered in their faith and both received only praise and encouragement. The other five existed in varying states of disrepair and each was urged to repent. Their individual strengths were acknowledged by the Lord, but their weaknesses were clearly delineated. Perhaps it could be compared to being called into the boss's office for a performance review that starts out with a rundown of what you're doing right, but then the other shoe drops and it quickly becomes clear that if you don't do some things differently you will soon be looking for a new job. Among the messages to those who were falling short of God's expectations were a couple of glaring common denominators.

In three instances, there was a lack of passionate love for God. Ephesus had abandoned her first love; Sardis had a reputation of being an alive and happening place, but was really dead; Laodicea was neither hot or cold, and there's not a lot of passion in any lukewarm relationship. Sounds a lot like Paul's teaching a few pages back regarding the fact that God desires 100% of our devotion rather than some lesser degree of split affection, doesn't it? Sounds like adultery against the Bridegroom.

And then we come to Pergamum and Thyatira. Now what did they do that bothered the Lord so much? Sadly, the same thing all of us have most likely been guilty of at some point in our lives—compromise. They tolerated false teachings and condoned unrighteous behaviors, not the least of which was sexual immorality, which again is akin to adultery against the Lord as well as false wisdom/blasphemy against the glorious ones.

What has changed between those first century churches and those of today? Sadly, not a lot. We live in a society that encourages tolerance of anything and everything, because to be intolerant would be unkind or unfair. No wonder that Jesus and His followers are so unpopular in many circles! He is well known to be a stumbling block and a rock of offense[4] to those who do not receive Him, and He said:

> *Do you think that I have come to give peace on earth? No, I tell you, but rather division.*[5]

The good news is that the remedies remain the same for the Church today as they did then, with repentance coming first. The words spoken to Ephesus are truly frightening:

> *Remember therefore from where you have fallen; repent, and do the works you did at first. If not, I will come to you and remove your lampstand from its place, unless you repent.*

How fortunate for all of us that we can depend on God's truth regarding the result of repentance:

> *Repent therefore, and turn back, that your sins may be blotted out, that times of refreshing may come from the presence of the Lord, and that he may send the Christ appointed for you, Jesus...*[6]

> *If we confess our sins, he is faithful and just to forgive us our sins and to cleanse us from all unrighteousness.*[7]

There's another common denominator among all seven letters; at the end of each are the exact, same words:

> *He who has an ear, let him hear what the Spirit says to the churches.*[8]

Or, as The Passion Translation (TPT)[9] reads:

> *The one whose heart is open let him listen carefully to what the Spirit is saying now to all the churches.*

It's abundantly clear that all seven of these churches were engaged in a spiritual war, as are we, and the lesson we should take away to use as we engage the enemy is two-fold. First, repent of our iniquities; and second, we <u>must</u> listen to and follow the lead of the Holy Spirit. If we do, we will not only be equipped for the battle but will also receive all of the amazing blessings that were promised to the seven churches if they became overcomers:

> *To the one who conquers I will grant to eat of the tree of life, which is in the paradise of God...The one who conquers will not be hurt by the second death...To the one who conquers I will give some of the hidden manna, and I will give him a white stone, with a new*

name written on the stone that no one knows except the one who receives it...The one who conquers and who keeps my works until the end, to him I will give authority over the nations, and he will rule them with a rod of iron, as when earthen pots are broken in pieces, even as I myself have received authority from my Father. And I will give him the morning star...The one who conquers will be clothed thus in white garments, and I will never blot his name out of the book of life. I will confess his name before my Father and before his angels...The one who conquers, I will make him a pillar in the temple of my God. Never shall he go out of it, and I will write on him the name of my God, and the name of the city of my God, the new Jerusalem, which comes down from my God out of heaven, and my own new name...The one who conquers, I will grant him to sit with me on my throne, as I also conquered and sat down with my Father on his throne.[10]

As conquerors, we can rule and reign with Christ, in Whom all this come together. Colossians 1 15-20 TPT well illustrates His supremacy and the truth that we can be reconciled to Him:

He is the divine portrait, the true likeness of the invisible God, and the first-born heir of all creation. For through the Son everything was created, both in the heavenly realm and on the earth, all that is seen and all that is unseen. Every seat of power, realm of government, principality, and authority—it was all created through him and for his purpose! He existed before anything was made, and now everything finds completion in him. He is the Head of his body, which is the church. And since he is the beginning and the firstborn heir in resurrection, he is the most exalted One, holding first place in everything. For God is satisfied to have all his fullness dwelling in Christ. And by the blood of his cross, everything in heaven and earth is brought back to himself—back to its original intent, restored to innocence again!

The entire Church should be standing to applaud Jesus for His State of the Church address!

---

[1] https://bible.org/article/interpretive-models-book-revelation-whole

[2] Galatians 1:6-7

[3] 1 Peter 1:1

[4] 1 Peter 2:8

[5] Luke 12:51

[6] Acts 3:19-20

[7] 1 John 1:9

[8] Revelation 2:7,11,17,29; 3:6,13,27

[9] Scripture quotations marked TPT are from The Passion Translation®. Copyright © 2017, 2018 by Passion & Fire Ministries, Inc. Used by permission. All rights reserved. ThePassionTranslation.com.

[10] Revelation 2:8,11,17,26-28; 3:5,12,21

CHAPTER FIFTEEN

COUNTERING DECEPTION WITH TRUTH

The second paragraph of the United States *Declaration of Independence*[1] begins with the famous phrase, "We hold these truths to be self-evident…" In much the same way, there are two truths that should be self-evident to anyone who reads the Bible. First, God is truth:

> *The sum of your word is truth, and every one of your righteous rules endures forever.*[2]

> *And the Word became flesh and dwelt among us, and we have seen his glory, glory as of the only Son from the Father, full of grace and truth… For the law was given through Moses; grace and truth came through Jesus Christ.*[3]

> *Jesus said to him, "I am the way, and the truth, and the life.*[4]

> *When the Spirit of truth comes, he will guide you into all the truth, for he will not speak on his own authority, but whatever he hears he will speak, and he will declare to you the things that are to come.*[5]

Second, as we've already seen, Satan is a liar; and deception is the name of his game:

> *Why do you not understand what I say? It is because you cannot bear to hear my word. You are of your father the devil, and your will is to do your father's desires. He was a murderer from the beginning, and does not stand in the truth, because there is no truth in him. When he lies, he speaks out of his own character, for he is a liar and the father of lies.*[6]

And the great dragon was thrown down, that ancient serpent, who is called the devil and Satan, the deceiver of the whole world—he was thrown down to the earth, and his angels were thrown down with him.[7]

Clearly, the devil has used deception from those first lies spoken to Eve in the Garden of Eden to the ones he spews into our minds every day, all in his already-failed quest to defeat Almighty God. Jesus put an end to that endeavor at the Cross; His personal examples and teachings throughout the Gospels reflect biblical truths on which we can depend.

Our freedom, our deliverance, our healing rests in His truth; but the enemy is skilled in twisting that truth, convoluting it in imaginative ways that boggle our minds. Satan's tactics are nothing less than military deception, which refers to attempts to mislead opposing forces during battle; this is usually accomplished by means of psychological operations, information warfare, visual deception and various other methods to create and/or amplify an artificial fog of war.[8] In other words, lying (disinformation) overlaps with psychological warfare in order to cause an opponent to hesitate when confronted with the truth. There can be no question that one of the most effective weapons any Christian can wield is God's Word, the truth that is part of the full armor of God:

Therefore take up the whole armor of God, that you may be able to withstand in the evil day, and having done all, to stand firm. Stand therefore, having fastened on the belt of truth, and having put on the breastplate of righteousness, and, as shoes for your feet, having put on the readiness given by the gospel of peace. In all circumstances take up the shield of faith, with which you can extinguish all the flaming darts of the evil one; and take the helmet of salvation, and the sword of the Spirit, which is the word of God, praying at all times in the Spirit, with all prayer and supplication.[9]

When the Continental Congress wrote the *Declaration of Independence*, they penned these words:

> The history of the present King of Great Britain is a history of repeated injuries and usurpations, all having in direct object the establishment of an absolute Tyranny over these States.

Next, they listed all of the abusive tactics of the king, and formally declared their independence from Britain. As we declare our own independence from the spiritual enemy's tyrannical rule, we can also recognize the enemy's lies and combat them with God's truth. To that end, we have prepared a list of common deceptions as contrasted with God's truths (to be found in Appendix 2), neither of which is conclusive by any stretch of the imagination. Hopefully, it will 'whet your whistle' to research God's biblical truth in areas of doubt in your own lives.

---

[1] http://www.ushistory.org/declaration/document/

[2] Psalm 119:160

[3] John 1:14,17

[4] John 14:6a

[5] John 16:13

[6] John 8:43-44

[7] Revelation 12:9

[8] https://en.wikipedia.org/wiki/Military_deception

[9] Ephesians 6:13-18a

CHAPTER SIXTEEN

A NEW DECLARATION

After the *Declaration of Independence* was unanimously approved in 1776, the *Articles of Confederation and Perpetual Union*[1] were developed and approved by the Second Continental Congress; this document began the process of establishing the standards by which the new United States of America would choose to live. The ensuing American Revolution would rage on for years, with tremendous loss on both sides. It was neither the first war nor the last, for nation has risen against nation throughout recorded history, and wars and rumors of wars will continue until the Day of the Lord.[2] But a much larger war has been raging since the first act of rebellion against God in the Garden of Eden; it's a war that knows no physical boundaries; it's the war of which we've been writing; it's the all-out spiritual conflict in which Satan and his followers are desperately trying to wrest all power and control over creation from the Creator. Regardless of the fact that it's a battle-already-lost for the enemy, we are still caught in the midst of its skirmishes throughout our lives here on earth. Perhaps we would be wise to take a page from the playbook of those early American colonists and declare our independence from the tyranny of evil. It might go something like this:

I hold these truths to be self-evident:

> All men are created in the image of God,[3] and are formed according to His perfect design.[4]

> God willingly gave His only begotten Son, the Lord Jesus Christ, that all who believe in Him shall not die, but will live with Him eternally.[5]

> It is the unalienable right of Christians to reject the oppressive and destructive rule of Satan, and to choose the life and liberty that is available through God's grace by

faith in the One Who is both the only begotten Son of God and the Son of Man, Jesus Christ.[6]

Therefore, I choose to:

Engage in the battle and follow my Commander-in-Chief, the Lord Jesus Christ.[7]

Seek Him first.[8]

Trust in God's perfect love instead of fear.[9]

Remain on alert against the wiles of the enemy.[10]

Persevere, overcome and endure.[11]

Own my identity as a revealed son of God instead of accepting any false identity the enemy has assigned to me.[12]

Practice oneness with God through faith instead of separation from Him through doubt and unbelief.[13]

Seek unity within myself and within the Body of Christ rather than division and disunity.[14]

Believe God's truth over the enemy's lies, especially that God is good and His loving-kindness endures forever.[15]

Reject false wisdom and embrace truth.[16]

I do this because, contrary to the enemy's lies, God's truth is:

God raised the Lord and will also raise us up by his power… [and] he who is joined to the Lord becomes one spirit with him… Or do you not know that your body is a temple of the Holy Spirit within you, whom you have from God? You are not your own, for you were bought with a price. So glorify God in your body.[17]

---

[1] https://en.wikipedia.org/wiki/Articles_of_Confederation

[2] Matthew 24:6

[3] Genesis 1:26-27

[4] Psalm 139:13-16

[5] John 3:16

[6] Joshua 24:14-15

[7] Ephesians 6:10-20; 2 Corinthians 10:3-5

[8] Matthew 6:33

[9] 1 John 4:18

[10] 1 Peter 5:8, 1 Corinthians 16:13

[11] James 1:25; 1 John 5:4-5; Romans 5:3-4

[12] John 1:12, 3:1-2

[13] Colossians 2:6-15

[14] Galatians 3:26-28; Ephesians 4; 1 Corinthians 12:12-13

[15] 2 Thessalonians 2

[16] John 8:32

[17] 1 Corinthians 6: 14, 17, 19-20

CONCLUSION

During November 2018, Persis Tiner[1] received a rhyme that sums up well the enemy's battle strategy versus God's winning remedy:

> Whirl winds, whirl winds, whirl winds
> Chaos here, and chaos there
> Running freely most everywhere
> Look to the right
> Look to the left
> What do you see?
> Chaos, chaos; that's what you see
> Now, look at Me
> Concentrate, and look square at Me
> This is where you'll find peace and grace
> Peace to weather the storm you'll find
> Grace to overcome and allow you to walk in the victory
> I have already won

Then in June 2019, Persis had another word; this one of tremendous hope:

> A fire, a fire, a fire
> A sword, a sword, a sword
> A sword, a fire (x3)
>
> And people think that I don't care
> And people think I'm unaware
> But the sword, the flaming fire
> And to those who have turned away
> And to those who have shut their ears
> And to those who have shut their eyes
> And to those who have closed their hearts
> I am coming with a flaming sword

Dear Lord Jesus (x3)

Ah, but for My people
Now you shall lie down and sleep and awake in safety
For I will surround you with my glory
Even though the dark powers prowl around you will not
be afraid

For the Lord alone is my savior

I am your Savior
I will rescue you

Thank You Father
Praise You Jesus
Praise You Lord
Thank You, Thank You, for You make everything right

The enemy will never cease to wield every weapon at his disposal until Jesus returns; but in the midst of the ongoing war between God's righteousness and the vilest evil, the Christian can not only rest in the Lord's amazing promises, but can also do serious damage to the enemy agenda. This is the battle for men's souls, and it will not last forever. A day is coming, much sooner than later, like a thief in the night; it is a day when our Victorious Risen Lord, Jesus Christ, will be evident to all.

Therefore God has highly exalted him and bestowed on him the name that is above every name, so that at the name of Jesus every knee should bow, in heaven and on earth and under the earth, and every tongue confess that Jesus Christ is Lord, to the glory of God the Father.[2]

---

[1] Persis Tiner is a prayer minister and a long-time friend of Aslan's Place; her prophetic wisdom and her faith under fire is an inspiration to all who know her; she is a true warrior

[2] Philippians 2:9-11 ESV

APPENDIX 1

PRAYER TO ABOLISH FEAR

Father, I come as your child, your heir, to repent on behalf of my generational line and myself for all of us who have failed to recognize our position and authority in Christ Jesus, choosing to be intimidated by fear rather than trusting you to be sufficient for all of our needs. Please forgive us for all of the times that we have set our eyes on the cares of the world instead of seeking You first.[1]

I repent for any instance in which we have frightened others through words or actions, becoming fear mongers who spread false teachings[2] and the deceitfulness of the world.[3] I now declare the truth that You, Lord, are my light and my salvation; of whom shall I be afraid? You are the strength of my life so whom should I fear?[4] You are my hiding place, my deliverer and protector,[5] and I choose now to take up the full armor of God[6] and use all of the weapons you put at my disposal to resist fear, knowing that it must flee in the face of faith.

In times when I am tempted to be afraid, I now choose to be strong and to let my heart take courage[7] as I wait for You. I choose to change my thinking and set my mind on things above,[8] looking to You as my deliverer, for I am persuaded that nothing in any physical or spiritual dimension is able to separate me from Your love.[9]

Father, Lord Jesus, Holy Spirit; You are my perfect love and I trust You now to cast fear out of my life according to your promise,[10] and I ask for a seven-fold return through the blood of Jesus of all that the enemy has stolen from me through fear and all of its by-products; I ask for your joy to well up within me and bubble over onto everyone I encounter; I boldly ask for the gift of faith to live with the assurance of things hoped for and the conviction of things not seen,[11] faith to move the mountains in my life and to live in victory through Christ Jesus.

I declare that this is the foundation of my faith; God is real, His Word is true; Jesus said it so I believe it, and I must always seek Him first. My life is His; He is my refuge and strength, my place of rest, my peace and my hope; He meets my every need. With Him on my side, I willingly choose to join the battle!

---

[1] Matthew 6:33

[2] Matthew 7:15

[3] Matthew 13:22, Acts 20:29

[4] Psalm 27:1

[5] Psalm 91

[6] Ephesians 6:10-17

[7] Deuteronomy 31:6

[8] Colossians 3:2

[9] Romans 8:38-39

[10] 1 John 4:18

[11] Hebrews 11:1

APPENDIX 2

THE GODS OF THE PEOPLES

ARTEMIS	DAGON	BEELZEBUB (BAAL PRINCE)
Identities:	**Identities:**	**Identities:**
Mother (Anti Holy Spirit)	Son (Anti Son of God)	Father (Anti God the Father)
Ceres (Greek pig goddess)	Zeus	Father of Child
Plutus (Greek)	Nimrod	Husband of Mother
Ishtar (Phoenician)	Bacchus	Club Symbol, meaning to break into pieces
Astarte (Canaanite)	Ninus	Gorth
Jezebel	Bel	Janus (Roman god of confusion)
Venus (Roman)	Tammuz	Nebo (Isaiah 46:1)
Mermaid (Icelandic)	Balder (Iceland)	Bel (Isaiah 46:1)
Sacti (Indian)	Ishwara (Indian)	Baal (bull)
Sacca (Assyrian)	Vishnu (Indian)	Hermes (Roman)
Isis (Egyptian)	Hercules	Kronos (Greek)
Phea (Greek)	Osiris (leopard, calf)	
Diane	Centaur: half horseman	
Hestia	Kissos	
Proserpine	Orion	
Diana (Roman)	Jupiter	
Ashtoreth (Canaanite)	Mercury	
	Cupid	
	Shing Moo (Chinese)	
	Buddha	
	Mars	
	Neptune (sea god)	

ARTEMIS	DAGON	BEELZEBUB (BAAL PRINCE)
Manifestation:	**Manifestation:**	**Manifestation:**
Hands	Chest	Forehead
Eyes		Shoulders
		Thighs
Purpose:	**Purpose:**	**Purpose:**
Control creative emotions	Control will	Mind control
Deforms	Control ideas	Splitting
Distorts	Confusion	
Retards	Destruction	
Rejects creativity	Root: embarrassment covering over emotions	
Results in anxiety		
Dyslexia		
Miscarriage		
Lack of sleep		
Arthritis		
Stress		
Itching		
Scratching		
Depression		
Black hole vortex		

APPENDIX 3

DECEPTION VERSUS GOD'S TRUTH

Common Lies of the Enemy	God's Perfect Truth According to His Word
God doesn't care.	*Do not be afraid of them, for I am with you to deliver you, declares the Lord." (Jeremiah 1:8* *...casting all your anxieties on him, because he cares for you. (1 Peter 5:7)*
You can save yourself for you alone control your destiny.	*John answered, "A person cannot receive even one thing unless it is given him from heaven. (John 3:27)* *The plans of the heart belong to man, but the answer of the tongue is from the Lord. (Proverbs 16:1)*
God can't/won't use you.	*For we are his workmanship, created in Christ Jesus for good works, which God prepared beforehand, that we should walk in them. (Ephesians 2:10)* *...for it is God who works in you, both to will and to work for his good pleasure. (Philippians 2:13)*
Satan, or the devil, is just a myth and not a literal evil threat.	*Be sober-minded; be watchful. Your adversary the devil prowls around like a roaring lion, seeking someone to devour. (1 Peter 5:8)*
Any choice one makes is acceptable because God gave us freedom of choice.	*No one can serve two masters, for either he will hate the one and love the other, or he will be devoted to the one and despise the other. (Matthew 6:24a)*

Common Lies of the Enemy	God's Perfect Truth According to His Word
Appearances and what others think of you are very important to God.	*But the Lord said to Samuel, "Do not look on his appearance or on the height of his stature, because I have rejected him. For the Lord sees not as man sees: man looks on the outward appearance, but the Lord looks on the heart."* (1 Samuel 16:7)
Sexual activities outside marriage, as well as homosexuality, and other traditional sexual taboos should be considered normal and acceptable; they are not sinful behaviors.	*For this is the will of God, your sanctification: that you abstain from sexual immorality; that each one of you know how to control his own body in holiness and honor, not in the passion of lust like the Gentiles who do not know God; that no one transgress and wrong his brother in this matter, because the Lord is an avenger in all these things, as we told you beforehand and solemnly warned you. For God has not called us for impurity, but in holiness. Therefore whoever disregards this, disregards not man but God, who gives his Holy Spirit to you.* (1 Thessalonians 4: 3-8)
God cannot be trusted.	*The saying is trustworthy, for...if we are faithless, he remains faithful—for he cannot deny himself.* (2 Timothy 2:11a, 13)
You're too bad to be forgiven by God.	*For God so loved the world, that he gave his only Son, that whoever believes in him should not perish but have eternal life. For God did not send his Son into the world to condemn the world, but in order that the world might be saved through him. Whoever believes in him is not condemned, but whoever does not believe is condemned already, because he has not believed in the name of the only Son of God.* (John 3:16-18)

Common Lies of the Enemy	God's Perfect Truth According to His Word
Satan is stronger than God.	*And I heard a loud voice in heaven, saying, "Now the salvation and the power and the kingdom of our God and the authority of his Christ have come, for the accuser of our brothers has been thrown down, who accuses them day and night before our God. (Revelation 12:10)*
There is no such thing as absolute truth; each person can create their own truth.	*See to it that no one takes you captive by philosophy and empty deceit, according to human tradition, according to the elemental spirits of the world, and not according to Christ. (Colossians 2:8)*
Morality is defined culture, not the Bible, so we can do whatever we want and are not guilty of sin, which is an antiquated idea.	*If we say we have no sin, we deceive ourselves, and the truth is not in us, If we confess our sins, he is faithful and just to forgive us our sins and to cleanse us from all unrighteousness. If we say we have not sinned, we make him a liar, and his word is not in us. (1 John 1:8-10)*
Happiness and well-being are God-given rights.	*I have said these things to you, that in me you may have peace. In the world you will have tribulation. But take heart; I have overcome the world. (John 16:33)*
This physical life is all there is, so the here-and-now is all that counts.	*And just as it is appointed for man to die once, and after that comes judgment... (Hebrews 9:27)* *Jesus said to her, "I am the resurrection and the life. Whoever believes in me, though he die, yet shall he live, and everyone who lives and believes in me shall never die. (John 11:25-26a*

Common Lies of the Enemy	God's Perfect Truth According to His Word
You will always have plenty of time to repent before you die.	*For he says, in a favorable time I listened to you, and in a day of salvation I have helped you." Behold, now is the favorable time. Now is the day of salvation. (2 Corinthians 6:2)* *As it is said, "Today, if you hear his voice, do not harden your hearts as in the rebellion." (Hebrews 3:15)*
God no longer heals or performs miracles.	*Jesus Christ is the same yesterday and today and forever. (Hebrews 13:8)*
God is a vengeful tyrant who expects perfection.	*The saying is trustworthy and deserving of full acceptance, that Christ Jesus came into the world to save sinners, of whom I am the foremost. But I received mercy for this reason, that in me, as the foremost, Jesus Christ might display his perfect patience as an example to those who were to believe in him for eternal life. (1 Timothy 1:15-16)*
God will always make exceptions for good people.	*"Not everyone who says to me, 'Lord, Lord,' will enter the kingdom of heaven, but the one who does the will of my Father who is in heaven. On that day many will say to me, 'Lord, Lord, did we not prophesy in your name, and cast out demons in your name, and do many mighty works in your name? And then will I declare to them, 'I never knew you; depart from me, you workers of lawlessness.'" (Matthew 7:21-23)*
Jesus has been gone so long that we can't expect him to come back after all this time.	*Be patient, therefore, brothers, until the coming of the Lord. See how the farmer waits for the precious fruit of the earth, being patient about it, until it receives the early and the late rains. You also, be patient. Establish your hearts, for the coming of the Lord is at hand. (James 5:7-8)*

Common Lies of the Enemy	God's Perfect Truth According to His Word
God is a killjoy who doesn't want people to enjoy life.	*There is nothing better for a person than that he should eat and drink and find enjoyment in his toil. This also, I saw, is from the hand of God, for apart from him who can eat or who can have enjoyment? (Ecclesiastes 2:24)*
You can only believe in what you can see; scientific proofs are required for truth.	*Now faith is the assurance of things hoped for, the conviction of things not seen. For by it the people of old received their commendation. By faith we understand that the universe was created by the word of God, so that what is seen was not made out of things that are visible. (Hebrews 11:1-3)*
There are some things that are so bad that you cannot forgive others.	*For if you forgive others their trespasses, your heavenly Father will also forgive you, but if you do not forgive others their trespasses, neither will your Father forgive your trespasses. (Matthew 6:14-15)* *...bearing with one another and, if one has a complaint against another, forgiving each other; as the Lord has forgiven you, so you also must forgive. (Colossians 3:13)*
Don't worry if you don't get everything right in this lifetime because you will be re-born into as many lives as you need to become perfect.	*And just as it is appointed for man to die once, and after that comes judgment. (Hebrews 9:27)* *For the wages of sin is death, but the free gift of God is eternal life in Christ Jesus our Lord. (romans 6:23)*
God can't/won't use you.	*Now there are varieties of gifts, but the same Spirit; and there are varieties of service, but the same Lord; and there are varieties of activities, but it is the same God who empowers them all in everyone. To each is given the manifestation of the Spirit for the common good. (1 Corinthians 12:4-7)*

Common Lies of the Enemy	God's Perfect Truth According to His Word
Dreams are just flights of the imagination while asleep and are not important.	*For God speaks in one way, and in two, though man does not perceive it. In a dream, in a vision of the night, when deep sleep falls on men, while they slumber on their beds, then he opens the ears of men and terrifies them with warnings, that he may turn man aside from his deed and conceal pride from a man; he keeps back his soul from the pit, his life from perishing by the sword. (Job 33:14-18)* *And in the last days it shall be, God declares, that I will pour out my Spirit on all flesh, and your sons and your daughters shall prophesy, and your young men shall see visions, and your old men shall dream dreams. (Acts 2:17)*
God doesn't care.	*In this the love of God was made manifest among us, that God sent his only Son into the world, so that we might live through him. (1 John 4:9)*
All faiths/religions are valid because there are many paths to God.	*Jesus said to him, "I am the way, and the truth, and the life. No one comes to the Father except through me. (John 14:6)* *Enter by the narrow gate. For the gate is wide and the way is easy that leads to destruction, and those who enter by it are many. 14 For the gate is narrow and the way is hard that leads to life, and those who find it are few. (Matthew 7:13-14)*
You can choose your sex if you don't like your biological identity.	*So God created man in his own image, in the image of God he created him; male and female he created them. (Genesis 1:27)*

Common Lies of the Enemy	God's Perfect Truth According to His Word
You can't change your behavior because you were born that way.	*Or do you not know that the unrighteous will not inherit the kingdom of God? Do not be deceived: neither the sexually immoral, nor idolaters, nor adulterers, nor men who practice homosexuality, nor thieves, nor the greedy, nor drunkards, nor revilers, nor swindlers will inherit the kingdom of God. And such were some of you. But you were washed, you were sanctified, you were justified in the name of the Lord Jesus Christ and by the Spirit of our God. (1 Corinthians 6:9-11)* *This is good, and it is pleasing in the sight of God our Savior, who desires all people to be saved and to come to the knowledge of the truth. For there is one God, and there is one mediator between God and men, the man Christ Jesus, who gave himself as a ransom for all, which is the testimony given at the proper time. (1 Timothy 2:3-6)*

Printed in Great Britain
by Amazon